Rethinking Gender and Sexuality in Childhood

A companion website to accompany this book is available online at:
http://education.kane.continuumbooks.com

Please type in the URL above and receive your unique password for access to the book's online resources.

If you experience any problems accessing the resources, please contact Bloomsbury at: info@continuumbooks.com

Also available in the *New Childhoods Series*

Rethinking Children and Families, Nick Frost
Rethinking Childhood, Phil Jones
Rethinking Children and Research, Mary Kellett
Rethinking Children, Violence and Safeguarding, Lorraine Radford
Rethinking Children's Rights, Sue Welch and Phil Jones

Also available from Bloomsbury

Whose Childhood Is It?, edited by Richard Eke, Helen Butcher and Mandy Lee
Thinking Children, Claire Cassidy

Rethinking Gender and Sexuality in Childhood

Emily W. Kane

New Childhoods Series

BLOOMSBURY

LONDON • NEW DELHI • NEW YORK • SYDNEY

Bloomsbury Academic
An imprint of Bloomsbury Publishing Plc

50 Bedford Square	175 Fifth Avenue
London	New York
WC1B 3DP	NY 10010
UK	USA

www.bloomsbury.com

First published 2013

British Library Cataloguing-in-Publication Data
A catalogue record for this book is available from the British Library.

ISBN: HB: 978-1-4411-3557-5
     PB: 978-1-8470-6082-2

Library of Congress Cataloging-in-Publication Data
A catalog record for this title is available from the Library of Congress.

Typeset by Newgen Imaging Systems Pvt Ltd, Chennai, India
Printed and bound in India

With heartfelt thanks to Emma Posner for outstanding
research assistance.

Contents

Introduction to New Childhoods series

The amount of current attention given to children and to childhood is unprecedented. Recent years have seen the agreement of new international conventions, national bodies established and waves of regional and local initiatives all concerning children.

This rapid pace has been set by many things. Demand from children themselves, from adults working with children, from governments and global bodies, new ideas and raw needs: all are fuelling change. Within and, often, leading the movement is research. From the work of multinational corporations designed to reach into the minds of children and the pockets of parents, through to charity driven initiatives aiming to challenge the forces that situate children in extreme poverty, a massive amount of energy is expended in research relating to children and their lives. Research can be seen as original investigation undertaken in order to gain knowledge and understanding through a systematic and rigorous process of critical enquiry examining 'even the most commonplace assumption' (Kellett, 2005, 9). This attention is not all benign. As Kellett has pointed out, the findings can be used by the media to saturate and accost, rather than support, under-12s who are seen as 'obese', for example, or to stigmatize young people by the use of statistics. However, research can also play a role in investigating, enquiring, communicating and understanding for the benefit of children and young people. Recent years have seen innovations in the focus of research, as political moves that challenge the ways in which children have been silenced and excluded result in previously unseen pictures of children's experiences of poverty, family life or community. The attitudes, opinions and lived experiences of children are being given air, and one of the themes within the 'New Childhoods' series concerns the opportunities and challenges this is creating. As this book will reveal, research is being used to set new agendas, to challenge ways of living and working that oppress, harm or limit children. It is also being used to test preconceptions and long held beliefs about children's lived experiences. In addition to the focus of research, innovations are being made in the way research is conceived and carried out. Its role in children's lives is changing. In the past much research treated children as objects, research was done on them, with the agenda and framework set purely by adults. New work is emerging where children create the way research is conceived and carried out. Children act as researchers, researchers work with questions formulated by children or work with children.

This series aims to offer access to some of the challenges, discoveries and work-in-progress of contemporary research. The term child and childhood is used within the series in line with Article 1 of the United Nations Convention on the Rights of the Child which defines 'children' as persons up to the age of 18. The books offer opportunities to engage with emerging ideas, questions and practices. They will help those studying childhood, or living and working with children to become familiar with challenging work, to engage with findings and to reflect on their own ideas, experiences and ways of working.

Phil Jones, Institute of Education, University of London

Part 1
Debates, Dilemmas and Challenges: The Background to Gender and Sexuality in Childhood

Introduction 1

Introduction and key questions

Researchers, practitioners and activists interested in children and childhood are increasingly focused on children's agency and children's rights. They are asking questions from the points of view of a diverse array of children and listening to children's voices as they aim to work in partnership with young people. Recent years have also seen new approaches to addressing issues of gender and sexuality, with attention to a wider range of gender identities and sexualities, sensitivity to variations by other social locations and national contexts, as well as greater recognition of the many arenas in which gendered patterns are constructed and resisted. It is the intersection of these two changing fields that is the topic of this book. This chapter introduces emerging approaches to children and childhood, as well as their implications for the study of gender and sexuality in childhood, by exploring three key questions:

- How do researchers and practitioners think about children and childhood today?
- How does this new approach shape the way we conceptualize childhood gender and sexuality in particular?
- How do these new ideas and approaches impact children's lives?

How do researchers and practitioners think about children and childhood today?

In stark contrast to the old adage that children should be seen and not heard, recent decades have witnessed an explosion of scholarship and action that assumes children should very much be heard: that their rights, autonomy and voices should play a pivotal role in research, policy and practice related to childhood. Children have been studied for centuries, with varying approaches taken by adult experts as they attempted to understand, care for, manage and even control young people. But as some authors in the interdisciplinary field now known as childhood studies point out, for much of history children have been viewed as some combination of innocents in need of adult protection or social problems in need of adult intervention (Shanahan, 2007). Either way, adults are assumed to know best, to know how to identify and serve the interests of both children and society by protecting innocent children and controlling problematic ones. Those involved in childhood studies today see children and childhood in a more nuanced manner, one that treats children as autonomous social actors who are not just in training for eventual participation in the adult world but are already active participants in their own peer worlds and the broader, multigenerational social world as well. Children are not simply blank slates upon which adults inscribe their influence, lessons and directions. They are resourceful agents, with their own interests and informed first-hand knowledge, who recreate and refine the social world rather than just passively accepting it as it is passed down by adults. Sociologist of childhood Corsaro (2005, 18–19) has coined a term that captures this outlook effectively: interpretive reproduction.

> The term interpretive captures the innovative and creative aspects of children's participation in society . . . children create and participate in their own unique peer cultures by creatively taking or appropriating information from the adult world to address their own peer concerns. The term reproduction captures the idea that children are not simply internalizing society and culture, they are actively contributing to cultural production and change.

Along with this emphasis on children's agency, also central to contemporary approaches to childhood studies are children's autonomy and rights. Rather than assuming children's best interests are automatically met by allowing adults to make decisions for them, this perspective prioritizes the autonomy and rights of children as independent social actors. Considered in detail in another book in this series (Jones and Welch, 2010), this movement is clearly evident in the 1989 United Nations Convention on the Rights of the Child (UNCRC). As Jones and Welch (2010, 46) note, the UNCRC identifies 'the human rights to be respected and protected for every child under the age of 18 years', with those rights based on a set of guiding principles: 'non-discrimination, the best interests of the child as the primary consideration, survival and development of all children, and participation of children in decisions that affect them'. They emphasize the tension between rights and duties, and how these play out differently and contentiously in various national and cultural contexts, particularly in terms of the links between a rights framing and Western conceptions that tend to prioritize the individual apart from and over social obligations or duties. But across these tensions and contentions, Jones and Welch (2010) point to substantial evidence that attention to children's rights (or unfortunately in some cases just a 'rights veneer') has become a central feature of much policy, practice and scholarship.

This approach to thinking about children has a parallel in the way scholars and advocates are viewing childhood these days: not as a naturally fixed and clearly demarcated developmental and chronological period, but rather as a historically and culturally fluid social construction, a dynamic product of social processes that changes in concert with social forces and activist efforts.

At what ages and in what ways people should be considered children is a social question, one answered in varying and shifting ways at different times and in different places.

Key points: A note on the terms childhood, youth and adolescence

James and James (2008) note that some of those working with and studying children use the term 'youth' to refer to the latter end of what is socially recognized as child-hood, generally ages 13 to 18 (149). Acknowledging all of these terms as social constructs, this book uses children and childhood to refer to the full range of ages from birth to 18, and sometimes uses the term youth to refer to older children. Given the frequency with which the literature and practitioners refer to 'adolescents', that term appears too, encompassing the same age range. The term invokes a more bio-logical meaning, while this book's emphasis is on childhood as a social phenomenon. But the terms 'adolescent' and 'adolescence' are particularly common in the research literature on sexuality and sexual health, literatures often situated at the intersection of social science and more biologically oriented sciences, and thus the term is used most often when those topics are being considered.

A final point that must be emphasized in even a brief overview of the way children and childhood are understood today is the diverse array of experiences children have, and the diverse array of childhoods, across racial/ethnic groups, classes, genders, sexual orientations, nations, religions and levels of ability and disability. Bühler-Niederberger and Van Krieken (2008, 148), in a recent analysis of global influences on children and childhood, argue that 'the notion of children's agency should not be interpreted as meaning that children (are) . . . purely individualized actors. Rather, they act within the frame of social, economic and political structures that often limit the scope of possible action'. Inequalities in access to social resources and opportunities, globally or within a given nation or community, shape how children can execute their agency. These inequalities structure different patterns and possibilities for childhood across different social groups. Economic constraints might encourage child labour in one context, such as the patterns Jacquemin (2006) documents in the Ivory Coast, where domestic service by young girls is sometimes encouraged by parents in need of the income their daughters can produce. In other contexts, early marriage for girls might be dictated by religious traditions, such as the Hindu practices sometimes evident in rural

India that are described by Dubey and Dubey (1999), or by poverty and economic necessity, explored in a variety of Latin American nations by Galambos and Martínez (2007). Racial or ethnic discrimination might block opportunities for children of colour in yet another context. Such patterns shape not only children's experiences of childhood, but also whether and how their voices are heard in policy and in research. As Ali, Fazil, Bywaters, Wallace and Singh (2001) argue, for example, disabled children have been particularly absent from the scholarly literature, with research on their experiences based on data gathered from caregivers rather than children themselves; among such children, even more dramatic is the absence of attention to the unique experiences and needs of black and Asian disabled children in the United Kingdom. Throughout this book, many examples of research and practice that demonstrate how childhoods vary by factors such as race, ethnicity, immigration status, national context, ability, religion, economic status, gender and sexuality are considered.

How does this new approach shape the way we conceptualize childhood gender and sexuality in particular?

Chapter 2 offers a more detailed consideration of recent trends in scholarship and practice related to gender and sexuality, but a highly condensed preview is in order here. Throughout this book, gender and sexuality are considered together. While gender refers to the social categories marking males and females, and the variety of expectations, roles, opportunities and traits socially associated with each, sexuality refers to the closely related expectations, roles, opportunities and traits socially associated with sexual activity, sexual identity and sexual orientation. Like childhood studies, gender and sexuality studies has been marked by changes in recent decades, changes that intersect with and in some ways parallel those related to childhood studies.

- Increasing attention to the social construction of gender and sexuality categories.
- Emphasis on hearing the voices and respecting the autonomy of people disadvantaged by social hierarchies of gender and sexuality.
- Recognition of the wide diversity of gendered experiences across nations, racial and ethnic groups, social classes, religions, sexual orientations and abilities.

Key points: Gender and sexuality

The links between gender and sexuality are explored more fully in Chapter 2, but a few brief points are helpful for highlighting why they are considered together throughout this book.

- Many scholars interested in gender, including childhood gender, now argue that traditional gender categories are built in part through the construction of traditional sexual orientation categories, linked in the concept of heteronormativity (see Chapter 2).
- For example, Martin and Kazyak (2009) document how presumed heterosexuality and 'sexiness' are inseparable from the representation of femininity offered in animated children's movies produced in the United States and distributed internationally, a melding they refer to as 'heterosexiness' (see Chapter 6).
- And Renold (2007) investigates how UK primary school boys enact masculinity, concluding that even at young ages the social definition of a 'real boy' includes heterosexual orientation and presumed sexual interest in pursuing girls, a conclusion that fits well with a broader trend in the scholarly literature to recognise 'the embeddedness of gender and sexuality' (275) (see Chapter 5).

These examples indicate the importance of considering sexuality alongside gender, even in the earlier years of childhood. As the range of research documented throughout this book reveals, these connections are even more obviously apparent as youth move into the ages at which they are making decisions about sexual activity, sexual health and sexual risk and as gendered expectations shape the landscape of those decisions in important ways.

These changes are all the more notable in the context of exploring gender and sexuality in childhood. The growing concentration on children's rights, agency, autonomy, voice and diversity intersect both to increase and shift the focus on children's gendered worlds. With particular interest in how children's gender and sexuality are shaped by adult influence but also resisted, refined and reproduced within children's peer cultures, and with attention to a much broader range of gender identities and sexual orientations, research and practice related to gender and sexuality in childhood has taken new directions. From the family to schools and educational policy to mass media and marketing to the peer cultures children craft, with cross-cutting influences from government, non-governmental organizations (NGOs), business, medicine, sport, religious and cultural organizations and a range of advocacy groups of all stripes, the social worlds in which children's gender and sexuality are reproduced and resisted offer a wealth of intriguing topics that form the basis for this book.

How do these new ideas and approaches impact children's lives?

The impact of these new approaches goes far beyond the textbook page or the volumes of academic research journals. From infancy to adolescence, across the wide age range encompassed by the term childhood, a focus on children's agency, autonomy, rights and diversity has significant implications for how gender and sexuality play out in childhood. In UNICEF's (2010a) summary of the UNCRC, the heart of one relevant article of the convention is captured as follows:

> Article 2 (Non-discrimination): The Convention applies to all children, whatever their race, religion or abilities; whatever they think or say, whatever type of family they come from. It doesn't matter where children live, what language they speak, what their parents do, whether they are boys or girls, what their culture is, whether they have a disability or whether they are rich or poor. No child should be treated unfairly on any basis.

UNICEF (2010b) identifies gender discrimination as a particular obstacle to fulfilling children's rights, noting that they:

> Work to protect and promote the rights of all children, yet in the light of these gender inequalities the organization has developed specific responses to reach girls . . . to ensure basic education for all girls, health care for adolescent girls and the protection of girls from abuse and exploitation.

This foundational emphasis on non-discrimination, an approach that seeks to guarantee girls the same rights as boys, is only one kind of impact on children's lives. The UNCRC's emphasis on children's best interests and development, as well as on children's agency in asserting their rights and participation in decisions that affect them, link to complex policy and legal debates around the world, highlighting controversies such as those outlined in Table 1.1.

Table 1.1 Selected examples of tensions and controversies surrounding children's gender and sexuality-related agency, autonomy and rights

Relevant article/ author(s)	Location and controversy addressed	Tensions highlighted	Further explored in . . .
Langer and Martin (2004); Giordano (2007)	USA; UK Ethical tensions around psychiatric and hormonal/ surgical intervention for gender-atypical childhood behaviour, including the power of parents, health care practitioners and children themselves	The rights of children to avoid non-reversible interventions before they are old enough to legally consent to treatment, but also their rights to seek treatment before those ages, especially in the context of adult power over those decisions legally	Chapter 2
Hunt (2009)	Canada The age at which children should be granted the right to consent to sexual activity, including same-sex relationships	Children's rights to sexual self-determination; children's autonomy in seeking sexual activity; differential rights allowed to children interested in same-sex versus opposite-sex sexual relationships; adult desires to 'protect' children by denying their sexual desires and agency	Chapter 2
Jacquemin (2006)	Ivory Coast Tensions between rights-based rhetoric in development programmes that seek to protect girls who are domestic workers and the daily lived reality of those girls' experiences as workers	Children's right to protection from exploitation by parents, guardians and domestic service employers; children's autonomy as workers/ economic agents; the power of NGOs to define children's rights and opportunities	Chapter 4
Ezekiel (2006); Laborde (2006)	France Bans on religious attire in schools primarily affecting Muslim schoolgirls who wish to wear headscarves to school	Balancing the state's interest in promoting national identity with children's autonomy in selecting gendered religious attire	Chapter 5
Bryant (2010)	Australia Youth access to pornography on the internet	Youth autonomy and agency in relation to sexual exploration; adult desires to protect youth from unwanted, harmful or violent pornographic images	Chapter 6

The examples in Table 1.1, and more presented throughout this volume, sketch the contours of the social, political and economic structures that constrain and shape children's gender and sexuality. For example, political constraints shape the options available to youth seeking sexual relationships in Canada, as detailed in Hunt's (2009) analysis of law. And economic interests may lead to the exploitation of girls by family members or employers, a topic addressed by Jacquemin (2006). But along with constraints, these examples also foreground the agency with which a diverse array of children participate in shaping their own and other children's gender and sexuality. As practitioners, policymakers, activists and scholars increasingly view childhood in general, and children's gender and sexuality in particular, through the lens of children's rights, autonomy and agency, and do so with attention to their diversity, the landscape of possibilities for children and youth is widened. At the same time, remaining tensions are revealed.

The organization of this book is designed first to provide the background for an exploration of these tensions and controversies. Chapter 2 addresses more fully the idea of gender as a social construct, and other debates that are current among analysts, activists and policymakers working on gender and sexuality issues. The chapter then considers how those ideas play out in approaches to children's gender and sexuality. In Chapter 3, the focus shifts from broad outlines to a closer look at specific research studies and advocacy programmes, previewing the social domains investigated in Chapters 4–7: the family; schools; media; and peer cultures. The book ends with Chapter 8, a conclusion that ties together key arguments and research findings. Throughout all of these chapters, research is presented from around the world, with attention to the voices of children from a diverse range of backgrounds and scholarship from many fields: sociology, psychology, education, gender and sexuality studies and childhood studies. Clear identification of key questions and concepts, accessible summaries of research and interviews with researchers as well as activities round out the coverage in each chapter, offering the reader a chance to apply, question and explore further the many topics and issues covered.

2 Children's Gender and Sexuality: Issues and Debates Defined

Chapter Outline

Introduction and key questions

Work related to children's gender and sexuality, whether research, policy or practice, is shaped by the way both children/childhood and gender/sexuality are theorized and understood. In this chapter, recent trends in gender and sexuality studies are sketched. These include a shift away from primary focus on gender-role and socialization models and increased recognition of the social construction of gender on multiple levels, along with rising attention to sexuality. The literature is also characterized by increased attention to men and boys as well as women and girls, and emphasis on intersections of gender and sexuality with other forms of social inequality. These trends are considered in the context of their particular applications to questions of childhood gender and sexuality. This exploration is organized around four key questions:

- What does it mean to talk about gender as being 'socially constructed'?
- How has the study of gender been changing?
- Has the way we think about children's gender been changing too?
- What kinds of changes have taken place in approaches to children's sexuality?

What does it mean to talk about gender as being 'socially constructed'?

For some people, the first thought to come to mind when they think about gender is biological variations related to physiology and reproductive capacities, variations that in everyday terms we think of as defining boys and girls, men and women. But how much, and in what ways, do those variations translate into social understandings of gender? The answer has varied so much over time and across place that it is not possible to support the claim that biology determines gendered outcomes. Against a wide range of natural variation across individuals, social discourse constructs the apparent inevitability of only two sharply distinct and internally homogeneous categories we call males and females. We dress and ornament boys and girls differently, teach them to behave differently, offer them different opportunities and obstacles, treat them differently in a host of ways and emphasize gender to them as a socially important category. Then we interpret the resulting patterns of gendered identity, attributes and behaviours as confirmation that they were different to begin with. This is the what authors are referring to when they view gender as socially constructed, a set of outcomes shaped by social processes that take place in the home, school, workplace, community and politics.

These processes constrain both males and females, socially constructing a strict binary of two highly distinct categories and guiding people, sometimes gently but sometimes coercively, into one or the other. More often than not, the process especially constrains girls and women, creating inequalities in the distribution of valued social resources by gender. It is that attention to inequality, a signal characteristic of much recent scholarship and activism related to gender issues, that has prompted a fundamental shift in the terms used to talk about gender. The language of 'socialization' to 'gender roles', though still used, is far less ubiquitous than it once was, because it implies easily internalized preferences for socially assigned activities and tasks and thus directs our attention away from questions of resistance, social change and unequal distribution of rewards. Widely cited gender studies scholar Raewyn Connell (1995, 26) notes that the 'intellectual limits of the role perspective . . . have repeatedly been shown', limits she summarizes as including:

- the assumption that a biological dichotomy of two neatly-distinct categories, male and female, underlies the roles that are socially layered on, despite a lack of evidence for that assumption; as Connell puts it regarding research evidence of biological sex differences, 'their modest size would hardly register them as important phenomena if we were not already culturally cued to exaggerate them' (1995, 21);
- a tendency to overstate the degree to which men and women follow socially prescribed behaviours, reinforcing a homogenous definition that ignores resistance as well as variation within and across subgroups and change across time;
- a tendency to view men's and women's prescribed roles as complementary, and thus a 'fundamental difficulty in grasping issues of power' and a 'broad assumption of consent' (1995, 27); as she points out elsewhere, 'we do not speak of 'race roles' and 'class roles' because the exercise of power in these areas of social life is more obvious to (us)' (1987, 50);
- the assumption that the primary site at which gender plays out in social life is within the individual, as individuals internalize and then act out socially prescribed roles.

In the last two decades or so, the broader notion of gender as socially constructed at three distinct levels has offered an alternative approach, one that allows for individual-level internalization of gender expectations without relying on it alone to explain gendered outcomes. As Risman (1998, 29) notes, gender is 'socialized into our (individual) personalities, but it also sets the parameters for interactional expectations and is built into our social institutions'. She goes on to explain that 'interactional pressures and institutional design create gender and the resultant inequality, even in the absence of individual desires'. Interactional pressures come from the kind of routine interactions with other people that fill our daily lives. Even when we may not have internalized the social roles associated with our gender, we may perform in the way others expect us to just to avoid social costs. Institutional pressures are also important to gender scholars these days, as they recognize the ways in which social institutions construct gendered patterns. For example, institutionally enforced options for males and females within a military organization, where females might be barred from combat, reinforce gender differentiation and differential skills, constructing gendered outcomes even if the individuals within that organization enter it with similar interests and a willingness to ignore interactional pressures. Or the gendered wage gap, a pattern in which women tend to earn less than men globally, reinforces gender differentiation within individual households when heterosexual couples who become parents often 'choose' to have the female parent take time off for child care due to her lower average wages. This choice might be made due to internalized role preferences or interactional pressures, but even absent those, it might be made due to the institutional constraints of the wage gap, another level at which gender is socially constructed.

How has the study of gender been changing?

Along with this broadened understanding of how gender categories and gendered patterns are socially constructed, several other trends are apparent in social science scholarship on gender. Briefly identified here, each is considered with specific examples in the next key question, as our focus narrows in on children and childhood.

- Increasing acknowledgement that gender issues affect not just girls and women, but boys and men as well; Connell and other scholars of the social construction of masculinity have played an important part in this trend.
- Deepened recognition that gender intersects with other forms of inequality such as race and ethnicity, social class, ability and disability, religion and international inequalities, a recognition that forces analysts not to assume that all women or all men are similarly affected by gendered constraints.
- Emphasis not just on the binary categories of male and female, but also on the interconnected but distinct categories of gender identity and sexuality, and the fluidity of such categories that is revealed by studying intersexuality, transgendered people and a wide variety of sexual orientations.

Has the way we think about children's gender been changing too?

Recognizing both gender and childhood as social constructs, for example, Montgomery (2005, 478) observes that 'the centrality of gender in children's lives is such that the very length of childhood may be determined by gender rather than chronological age'. She goes on to explain by referencing the earlier ages at which girls relative to boys are expected to marry and take responsibility for a family in some nations and cultures. The literature documents the many ways in which children's daily lives are shaped by gender in a wide variety of cultural contexts. Table 2.1 offers just a few brief examples.

Along with a great number of research studies documenting continued gender differentiation, approaches to children's gender are widening and shifting in parallel, and sometimes overlapping and intersecting, with the ways the literature on gender among adults has shifted. Children's agency and autonomy in the gendering process is one such overlap. Just as gender scholars are moving away from reliance on one-way socialization models that assume smooth internalization of gender roles, childhood studies scholars are moving

Table 2.1 Select research findings on gender shaping children's daily lives

Author(s)	Location of research, age range of children and research method	Gendered pattern documented
Tenenbaum, Hill, Joseph and Roche (2010)	UK 3–8 year olds Picture drawing and recognition tasks	Even 3- to 4-year-old British children hold specific ideas about what boys and girls do, ideas that become increasingly conventional as they reach ages 7 or 8
Yu and Xie (2010)	China 9–12 year olds Survey data	Both boys and girls in China feel pressure to conform to gender expectations, and have higher self-esteem if they consider themselves gender typical
Cherney and London (2006)	USA 5–13 year olds Survey data on toy, television and other leisure preferences	Boys and girls have notably different preferences, which 'provide differential opportunities for the development of visual-spatial skills, achievement, initiative, self-regulation, and social skills' (717)
Kosminsky and Daniel (2005)	Brazil Various ages Ethnographic observation of play	Children in a low-income urban neighbourhood reveal deeply gendered patterns in their games, patterns strongly influenced by their parents

away from passive models of children and childhood. Thus, we find increasing attention to the active part children play in shaping gendered worlds in childhood. Examples of pioneering work in this area include Davies' (1989) analysis of how 3- and 4-year-olds respond to fairy tales that attempt to resist or refine gender stereotypes and Thorne's (1993) ethnography of gendered interactions in elementary schools. Davies found that despite her adult assumption that non-traditional gender narratives would open up new possibilities in the minds of her young participants, the children sometimes resisted these narratives, enjoying but also recasting them back into line with the more traditional narratives they already knew. Thorne's observation of older children also revealed their active agency, as many of the gendered boundaries that shaped, for example, playground life were actively constructed by the children, and within their peer cultures various breaches of those boundaries were allowed under circumstances dictated by the children themselves.

Key points: Children as active agents in the gendering process

As Davies (1989, 5) puts it in criticizing what was then called the 'sex-role socialization' approach (and is now more commonly called a gender-role socialization approach):

The child is taught her or his sex-role by, usually, one central adult, but is also 'pressed' into maintenance of that role by a multitude of others. . . . There is no room in this model for the child as active agent, the child as theorist, recognising for him or herself the way the social world is organised . . . (and) implicated in the construction and maintenance of the social world through the very act of recognizing it.

Thorne (1993, 3) offers a similar framing, noting that after spending a significant period of time 'hanging out' in an elementary school:

I increasingly became dissatisfied with the frameworks of gender socialization and gender development that organize most of the literature on the social construction of gender in children's lives. For one thing, the concept of socialization moves mostly in one direction . . . as an observer in schools, I have been impressed by the ways in which children act, resist, rework and create.

Interview with Bronwyn Davies about her research, past and present

Bronwyn Davies is currently a Professorial Fellow in the Graduate School of Education at The University of Melbourne in Australia, and works as an independent scholar.

Emily Kane:	Are you still working on issues related to childhood and gender?
Bronwyn Davies:	Yes, one of my current projects involves rewriting children's stories from a present-day feminist perspective and using them to engage in thinking through the relations between narrative and social change, and changing gender relations in particular. Another project is based on observations in Reggio Emilia inspired preschools in Sweden. Here my interest has turned to listening and to an ethics based on being open to the other in their difference. I have written several papers on this study that I will be drawing together as a book.
Emily Kane:	Thinking back, what surprised you the most about the process or results of the research reported in your 1989 book *Frogs and Snails and Feminist Tales*?
Bronwyn Davies:	I don't think of the book as having produced 'results' – it was more an exploration of a new way of thinking about gender and how we become gendered. It was while writing that book that I discovered poststructuralist theory and the new and surprising possibilities for thinking about gender that opens up. And preschool children themselves are always surprising. They have such interesting and unexpected things to say. What continues to be most surprising to me is the way in which the book has taken on a life of its own. It is translated into German and Spanish and more recently into Swedish and parts of it into Hindi. It gave rise to a study of Japanese preschool children and gender (Davies and Kasama, 2004). It has no intention of fading away into obscurity.
Emily Kane:	How does an emphasis on children's agency and autonomy continue to shape your research work today, over two decades after the first publication of *Frogs and Snails and Feminist Tales*?
Bronwyn Davies:	I continue to be fascinated by, and to explore, what it means to listen to children in such a way that I am open to being changed by what I hear. I think of research – and indeed any meeting with children – in terms of an encounter where each is open to the other, where each learns from the other and is open to being moved by the other. This interest will lie at the heart of my new book on preschool children.

Example of research: Children's agency and autonomy in the social construction of gender

Kosminsky and Daniel (2005) spent a year completing interviews with children and observing their play in a favela, or very low-income urban neighbourhood, in the Brazilian city of Marilia. Though they attend to the role of parents and other relatives in dictating some aspects of children's gendered play, such as mothers or grandmothers discouraging doll play for boys while they encourage it for girls, they also emphasize the actions of the children. They argue that 'street games enable the observer

⇨

to witness the gender relations developed by the children' (32). These autonomous, child-generated relations sometimes reinforce the constraints of gender divisions and stereotypes, but sometimes reconstruct those constraints. For example, Kosminsky and Daniel's observation notes document the ways in which the girls refined the doll play encouraged by their relatives: 'In their own world, little girls could play with dolls and create different situations for their games, such as the doll being a woman who worked in an office or a doctor' (34).

Reflections on the research

Activity

Kosminsky and Daniel's research is based on observations of childhood games. Think back to a game you played as a child, or to a childhood game you have witnessed, seen in movies or read in books. How does this game, either in its format or in the way you have seen it refined by children, reinforce or resist gender divisions and stereotypes? In Kosminsky and Daniel's terms, how does it facilitate your ability to think about 'the gender relations developed by the children'?

Kosminsky and Daniel (2005) also draw attention to the increasing focus on boys that characterizes the field. Like Thorne (1993) in a different country and a different decade, they argue that girls and boys face different responses if they cross into terrain traditionally reserved for the other. 'In conversations between mothers and sons, we noted that mothers often would not permit their sons to play with dolls with their sisters or neighbours. In contrast, mothers approved of their daughters playing soccer or playing with small carts' (34). They link this pattern to Thorne's (1993) previous findings in the United States, in which she documents that boys who tried to join in on girls' games were often rejected by girls and ridiculed by other boys, while some girls were able to successfully enter boys' games, as long as they were willing to play by the boys' rules. Though gender inequalities advantage boys and men in many ways, scholars increasingly recognize that social expectations for masculinity also narrow the range of options considered acceptable for boys and men in troubling ways.

Another point of overlap between the childhood and gender studies literatures is in the recognition of gender as a complex, multidimensional concept, not simply a binary of two fixed categories, male and female. Children's anatomy, gender identities and gender performance fall at many points along various continua, raising a range of complicated questions that are receiving more attention lately. In an article exploring how medical professionals and parents navigate the birth of a child with genital 'anomalies' that make it unclear how to answer that common question, 'is it a boy or a girl', Ahmed, Morrison and Hughes (2004, 847) note that 'gender has several aspects'. They go on to describe the range of categories some contemporary analysts identify.

- Gender assignment, or the gender that medical personnel dictate at birth;
- Gender role, or the expectations a given society or group holds for individuals assigned to each gender category;
- Gender identity, or the way an individual feels rather than what others assign or expect;
- Gender attribution, or the assumptions people make about another person's gender category in everyday life.

Though in many cases all four of these aspects line up, in some they do not, including cases in which the gender assignment at birth is difficult due to anomalies. Ahmed and colleagues argue for gender assignment to take place as early as possible in those cases, so that the infant can be socially recognized as a boy or girl. That position is held by many medical professionals but also challenged by advocates for these 'intersex' children, some of whom argue any such assignment and especially surgical alteration of genitalia should be delayed until the patient has reached the age of consent for their own medical procedures.

Similar issues arise in literature addressing significant levels of childhood gender atypicality, given that sometimes psychiatrists and psychologists wish to intervene and encourage more gender typical childhoods. Bioethicist Giordano (2007) comments that 'there are no agreed on international guidelines on the treatment of children and adolescents with atypical gender identity organisation' (366). Focusing on the United Kingdom, she argues that such guidelines are needed, and that they must incorporate ethical considerations, including the child's right to 'give valid informed consent to treatment' such as hormonal and surgical treatment if desired (366). This article highlights both the attention paid to a broad range of gender and sexual identities in childhood and the emphasis on children's rights to make autonomous decisions that often characterize the approaches taken today. Giordano argues, for example, that if a child wishes to receive hormonal treatment to delay the onset of puberty until he or she is old enough to consent to non-reversible surgery to transition from male to female or female to male, ethical guidelines should be established to allow for that. Langer and Martin (2004) offer a related argument in a different national context, criticizing the American Psychological Association's diagnostic category of 'gender identity disorder of childhood' (GIDC) as ethically problematic. They summarize the circumstances under which the diagnosis is applied to children, 'if they experience persistent discomfort with their assigned sex and they verbally or behaviourally express cross-gender identification on a regular basis' (5). Consistent with the pattern noted by Thorne (1993) as well as Kosminsky and Daniel (2005), Langer and Martin (2004) report that boys are six times as likely to be referred for treatment with this diagnosis, 'likely due to the greater social acceptance of nonconforming behavior among girls' (6). They conclude that there are serious ethical problems involved in any intervention to change a child's gender identity, an approach that seeks to grant autonomy and rights to the child rather than only adult authority figures. A detailed history of the creation of the psychological diagnostic category of GIDC is offered by Bryant (2006, 2008). Searching through archives and published research papers, and interviewing doctors, activists and researchers, he traces the movement away from defining homosexuality as a mental disorder and the parallel timing of the addition of the new diagnosis of GIDC. With this history as crucial context, he also 'examines some of the limitations of current debates over GIDC and points out new trends that hold the most promise for providing support to gender-variant children' (2006, 23).

Analysts of children's gender, like gender and childhood studies scholars generally, are also increasingly attentive to variations in gendered childhoods by race, socioeconomic class, ability and disability, religion and national context. In a review of scholarship on the relevance of gender to understanding childhood, Morrow (2006, 93) urges both researchers and practitioners to avoid 'assuming that there are some universal characteristics that apply to all girls and all boys', emphasizing that 'social differences do not operate in isolation, because social class, age, ethnicity, religion, and location intersect to influence children's childhoods and their gender identities'. This kind of attention is evident in the approach taken by advocacy groups and NGOs as well. UNICEF (2010b, 10), for example, acknowledges the variations in gendered experiences when they state that 'no group of girls and boys, or men and women, is entirely homogeneous. All include members of social sub-groups, defined by age, religion, race, ethnicity, economic status, caste, citizenship, sexual identity, ability/disability, and urban/rural locality'.

Example of research: Recognizing intersecting inequalities

Ali and colleagues (2001) offer a detailed review of UK research on disability in childhood. Drawing on examples from across 26 selected studies, the authors offer rich descriptions of occasions in which gender, ethnicity and disability intersect to shape a unique set of constraints.

- In one such case, a black, female youth with cerebral palsy did not receive culturally appropriate assistance with her hair care needs in a predominantly white boarding school. None of the staff knew how to comb or plait her hair, and made no effort to learn, requiring elaborate and painful detangling when she visited home during school vacations.
- In another case, Muslim parents with disabled children reported reluctance to use an available respite care centre because their religious preferences were not respected in the way staffing was organized in the centre, with male staff members caring for female children or care provided for boys and girls together when parents preferred segregation.

The authors also find that in many studies youth voices are heard only through adults with disabilities recollecting their childhood experience, a limitation they argue requires greater efforts to hear directly from children experiencing disability, with particular attention to a diversity of voices and backgrounds.

Reflections on the research

Intersecting inequalities will be emphasized throughout this book, and this study reminds us that children's lives are impacted not only by their gender, but also by the unique intersections they inhabit in terms of gender and other forms of inequality. For the children profiled in this article, the everyday experiences of disability are shaped by the intersections of gender, ethnicity and location.

Activity

Thinking about the two examples in the bullets above, briefly outline how staff supervising children with disabilities could better acknowledge the intersections of gender, ability/disability, ethnicity and culture, while also recognizing more fully children's autonomy and agency.

What kinds of changes have taken place in approaches to children's sexuality?

Another relatively new direction in childhood studies is greater recognition of children's sexuality. This includes attending to the harsh realities of sexual abuses such as child trafficking, child prostitution and child pornography, all areas in which UNICEF (2010b) and many other NGOs have established initiatives. Researchers are exploring the incidence and effects of childhood sexual abuse, as well as how both vary for boys versus girls. For example, analysis of Icelandic survey data conducted by Gault-Sherman and her colleagues (2009) documents that more teen girls than boys reported experiencing sexual abuse, and the psychological impacts of that experience varied by gender, with abused girls more likely to report depression and anxiety than abused boys. But in keeping with other trends in the field, childhood studies scholars also recognize children and youth as sexual beings with a diversity of cultures and backgrounds, and with agency, autonomy and rights not just to protection from sexual abuse but to sexual health, sexual education and voluntary sexual activity as well. Egan and Hawkes (2008, 360) highlight this point.

> The rights of children, as sexual subjects, are often singularly framed as the right of protection from sexual exploitation but rarely do these conversations turn toward the equally important right of sexual agency . . . The social recognition of children as sexual citizens is still ideologically tethered to what adults deem to be socially acceptable sexuality. (365)

Example of research: Sexual agency in childhood and youth

Canadian youth researcher Hunt (2009) investigates the legislative history surrounding sexual consent age limits in both UK and Canadian law, analysing the specific language and arguments used in legislative and legal documents as well as the specific rules enacted. On the basis of that analysis, he argues that youth sexuality is often framed in terms of protection rather than agency, and that limitations on the right to consent have been further differentiated in terms of male same-sex sexual behaviour, in that anal intercourse had an even higher age of consent. While anal intercourse occurs among heterosexual partners, and male same-sex sexual behaviour encompasses much more than just anal intercourse, Hunt argues that the differential age of consent was shaped by assumptions about anal intercourse being associated with male same-sex relationships.

- In the United Kingdom, this differentiation was removed in 2000; when the age of consent for anal intercourse was lowered to 16, the same age applied to other sexual activity, based on an argument for equality of treatment regardless of sexual orientation.
- According to Hunt, the same argument was not successful in Canada. After a legislative struggle ending in 2008, Canada's previous age of consent for sexual activity other than anal intercourse was raised from 14 to 16 but the age of consent for anal intercourse was left at 18. This still left a differential age of consent depending on sexual orientation and gender, thus constructing what is often assumed to be a male same-sex sexual activity as something from which youth need even more protection.

⇨

Example of research – Cont'd

As Hunt sums it up, this has implications for non-heterosexual youth, and for all youth. 'The age-of-consent regulation not only regulates youth sexual activity but also disempowers youth by defining them as unable to grasp the implications of their actions, thus reducing and constraining – if not at times wholly eliminating – recognition of their ability to consent' (29).

Reflections on the research

Age-of-consent regulations may protect children, but at the same time they offer a clear example of how children's sexual agency is constrained by the state, in ways that vary by nation and, within a nation, can also vary by the child's gender and sexuality.

Activity

Look back to the discussion of the institutional, interactional and individual levels of gender construction discussed earlier in this chapter. Hunt's findings document that age-of-consent legislation presents youth with an institutional constraint to their gender and sexuality. How might the age-of-consent legislative history in Canada and the United Kingdom also relate to or create gender constraints for youth at the interactional and individual levels?

Attention to youth sexual agency, including the agency of gay, lesbian and bisexual youth, extends to emphasis on sexual health and sexual education for youth from all backgrounds as well. Researchers and advocates are arguing that youth from all backgrounds and cultures have a right to adequate health care and information related to their sexual lives. Even a few samples document the trend.

- Rogers (2009) reviews policy and practice in relation to sexuality education for UK youth with learning disabilities, calling upon adults to respect the desire for sexual activity and intimacy among youth with disabilities by providing them with appropriate sex education in schools.
- According to the call for youth participation in the 2009 NGO Forum on Sexual and Reproductive Health and Development in Berlin, co-hosted by the German government and the United Nations Population Fund, 'Young people should no longer face the burden of insufficient access to information, services, support, choices and the right to decide on matters regarding their own bodies, especially their sexual and reproductive health and rights' (Global Partners in Action 2009).
- Hyde and colleagues (2010) explore obstacles that Irish parents report facing from their own adolescent children in response to parental attempts to provide information related to sexual health. The authors argue for the importance of understanding

these obstacles and the role of youth themselves in fostering the level of communication necessary for adequate home-based youth sexuality education.

- Bhana (2009, 165) analyses HIV/AIDS education in two different primary schools in Durban, South Africa, to document how 'discourses of childhood innocence make it difficult for teachers to provide comprehensive knowledge of sex, sexuality, and gender in the primary school "life skills" lessons', knowledge the author claims should be provided.
- Elia and Eliason (2010) document how lesbian, gay, bisexual and transgendered (LGBT) youth are silenced within both US and international sexuality education curricula, and argue that all students would benefit from a new approach more inclusive of the sexual health and sexual education needs of LGBT youth.

Sexuality is drawing the interest of childhood studies researchers for younger children as well. Martin and colleagues (2007) maintain that young children's 'sexual socialization' is a crucial topic for examination. They see it as important in terms of the cultural resources children will have in future sexual action 'as they navigate their way to sexual adulthood' (235) and as a logical outgrowth of childhood studies' emphasis on children as social actors in their own right. In addition, they argue that it will further our understanding of 'how heterosexuality is constructed' (235). This latter point highlights another site of intersection between the childhood and gender studies literatures, as scholars increasingly view sexual orientation categories, including heterosexuality, as social and historical constructions. Among social scientists, the term heteronormativity has been developed to capture the taken-for-granted assumption that people should be and are (or in the case of young children eventually will be) heterosexual. Gender studies scholars generally agree that heteronormativity not only reinforces the power of heterosexuals but that it also reproduces gender categories and gendered power. And those investigating heteronormativity in childhood have documented myriad ways in which gender and sexuality are simultaneously constructed in children's worlds. Take, for example, Renold's (2007) ethnographic work in educational settings. She details how performances of heterosexuality in 10- and 11-year-old boys' peer cultures are foundational to establishing a socially valorized masculine identity (see Chapter 7 for more details). As Martin and colleagues (2007) point out, this process extends back into pre-school settings as well, where play materials sometimes include a 'wedding box' of props for role play and Valentine's Day rituals often celebrate heterosexual imagery (251).

Example of research: Heteronormativity and the social construction of gender in children's worlds

In order to explore how childhood gender is constructed, Riggs (2008) conducted a content analysis of ten advice books for fathers of sons in Australia. He carefully sifted through the advice offered, and the assumptions made, about the 'average boy'. Based on that analysis, he argues:

- The assumptions made about the 'average boy' are not so much reflecting as actually constructing the meanings surrounding boyhood, and assumptions about sexuality are pivotal to what is expected of this average boy.
- These advice books are 'among the prime proponents and manufacturers of a highly normative understanding of masculinity and boyhood' (188).
- Fathers are encouraged to assume their young sons will be attracted to girls and to discourage any 'sissy' tendencies.
- The books' underlying assumptions about the 'average boy' and the naturalness of his attraction to girls are 'informed by a range of heteronormative and homophobic assumptions about boys and masculinity' (186).
- Presumed heterosexuality is recreated in tandem with fundamental notions of gender identity, not as two separate processes but as a single process in which part of the definition of being a boy is to be heterosexually oriented.

Reflections on the research

Parents clearly play an important role in teaching their children lessons about gender and sexuality. Riggs' article focuses on the potential power of fathers by addressing the messages they receive about what is normal and natural for boys, and considering how that may shape fathers' treatment of their sons.

Activity

How do you think Riggs' findings – that advice books for fathers reflect a presumed heterosexuality that is intertwined in a child's gender identity – relate to Davies' (1989) critique of 'sex role socialisation' theories discussed earlier in the chapter? How might what Riggs and Davies suggest be combined in thinking about the role of both parent and child in the gendering process?

From the basic argument that gender and sexuality are socially constructed, to more specific trends and patterns in scholarship from around the world and across disciplines, this chapter has offered a basic outline of issues and debates in the literature on gender and sexuality in childhood.

Chapter activities

Activity 1: Social construction of gender at various levels

This chapter discussed the notion that gender is socially constructed at the institutional, interactional and individual levels. Review the four examples of research spotlighted in this chapter and jot a few notes about the levels at which gender is reinforced, resisted or constrained in each. Remember that multiple levels can be at play in a given example.

	Individual	Interactional	Institutional
Kosminsky and Daniel			
Ali and colleagues			
Hunt			
Riggs			

Activity 2: Children's autonomy and gender identity

This chapter highlighted debates and research on 'intersex' children and childhood gender atypicality. Giordano (2007) emphasizes the ethical importance of a child's autonomy in decisions regarding treatment for gender atypicality. Should there be, as Giordano suggests, 'agreed on international guidelines on the treatment of children and adolescents with atypical gender identity organization' (366)? Choose a side on this debate and outline how you would support your argument. Make sure to incorporate the themes of this chapter, considering both childhood studies and gender studies approaches.

Summary

This chapter has:

- Discussed how a range of human variation is socially constructed into two, binary gender categories;
- Identified key trends and assumptions in contemporary scholarship and activism related to gender;

- Described trends and debates characterizing today's research and advocacy related to gendered childhoods;
- Explored how children's sexuality is also increasingly an area of interest for childhood studies practitioners and academics.

Further reading

Davies, B. (2011), 'Open listening: Creative evolution in early childhood settings', *International Journal of Early Childhood*, 43, 2, 119–32.

Recent article exploring the process of conducting research with children, by the author of other research cited in this chapter. See her author interview for more on her current work.

Turner, S. (1999), 'Intersex identities: Locating new intersections of sex and gender', *Gender & Society*, 13, 4, 457–79.

Analysis of case studies from the website of the 'Intersex Society of North America', exploring activism on behalf of intersex people and their demand for delay of surgical intervention until intersex children are old enough to consent.

Research details

Children's agency and autonomy in the social construction of gender

Peer-reviewed journal. The researchers (Kosminsky and Daniel, 2005) spent a year completing interviews with 7- to 10-year-old children and their families in 52 very low-income Brazilian households and then observing their toys and play, tape recording the interviews and taking detailed field notes.

Recognizing intersecting inequalities

Peer-reviewed journal. While many research examples throughout this book involve the authors collecting data through methods such as surveys, interviews, observation or experiments, Ali and colleagues' (2001) study involved a careful analysis of other people's research findings. The authors searched databases of UK research on disability in childhood, systematically selecting 26 existing research studies focused on children that also emphasize youth voices and perspectives.

Sexual agency in childhood and youth

Peer-reviewed journal. Hunt (2009) reviews the specific language deployed in debates surrounding the age of sexual consent in both UK and Canadian law. The analysis relies on the text of laws, as well as reports and testimony considered by legislators and the discourse used by those legislators themselves over decades in both the British Houses of Commons and Lords, and the Canadian Parliament.

Heteronormativity and the social construction of gender in children's worlds

Peer-reviewed journal. The author (Riggs, 2008) selected ten recent parenting advice books written specifically for fathers, about raising sons. The books were selected based on their wide availability in bookstores (determined using topic searches on major bookstore websites) and Australian libraries, as well as the frequency with which they are cited in various electronic citation indices used by scholars and journalists.

Part 2
An Interdisciplinary Overview of Recent Research and Scholarship

The Social Construction of Gender and Sexuality in Childhood, Key Research Issues and Findings

3

Chapter outline

Introduction and key questions

Having established central trends in childhood studies and gender studies in Chapters 1 and 2, this chapter moves on to introduce more specific themes within the literature on gender and sexuality in childhood. In keeping with the foundational view that gender is socially constructed, and that children are constrained by adult power but also are active agents in their own diverse social worlds, this chapter offers a preview of the remainder of the book by answering three key questions:

- Who are some of the key social actors involved in constructing childhood gender and sexuality?
- What role do children themselves play in constructing childhood gender and sexuality?
- What role does the state play in constructing gender and sexuality in childhood?

Who are some of the key social actors involved in constructing childhood gender and sexuality?

The social construction of children's gender and sexuality plays out in a variety of contexts, with many different individuals and social institutions involved. More detailed and specific exploration of some of the key players is offered in Chapters 4–6, which focus on the family, educational institutions and mass media. A few patterns and examples from each provide a brief introduction to how the scholarly literature highlights these three arenas as especially important.

The family is a good place to start, as most children begin their lives in some kind of family context. Within families, children are influenced by siblings, grandparents and a host of other relatives, but parents are a particularly common focus for researchers interested in childhood gender and sexuality.

Example of research: Styles of toy play with sons and daughters

Wood, Desmarais and Gugula (2002) observed experimental toy play sessions between adults and 2- to 6-year-old children in Canada, carefully selecting the toys offered to include some rated as traditional for boys, girls or both. The play sessions were followed by a questionnaire given to the adults about their perceptions of the desirability of each toy for boys or girls. Adults included the children's parents as well as other adults, with each child engaging in multiple play sessions. The researchers found that the adults in their study – both the child participants' parents and other adults – had broader definitions of which toys were appropriate for boys versus girls than prior studies had found. Instead of considering most toys suited to either girls *or* boys, they found a larger number suitable for both. They took this pattern as an indication of social change, with less gender differentiation in adult attitudes about appropriate toys for children. But even so, the researchers found that when given a choice in the actual play situation as opposed to the questionnaire, the adults, parents included, tended to play with gender-typed toys, especially for boys. Given the age of the children involved in the study, Wood and her colleagues also point out that the children themselves play a part in the process, recognizing the child as an active agent. As they note in their conclusion, 'the bidirectional nature of the interaction between adult and child during play may have modified the play situation' (48).

Reflections on the research

Activity 1

Think about your own memories of playing with toys as a child, and jot down some notes on how your toy preferences might have been shaped by parents or other adults, siblings and peers with whom you played, advertisements you saw and any other factors that come to mind.

Activity 2

Write a brief reflection on whether/how you think your memories demonstrate the 'bidirectional' adult–child interactions that the authors emphasize.

From routine toy preferences to more dramatic examples related to domestic violence and child labour, a great deal of research documents differential treatment by parents based on children's gender. Chapter 4 considers not only that research but also some of the constraints that shape parental treatment: family policy, international NGOs, medical and social services experts, economic scarcity and everyday pressures from friends, relatives and even strangers. The chapter also addresses research exploring the role of siblings as peer influences, how gender plays out in a diverse array of family types (including families from varying national, religious and cultural backgrounds as well as gay and lesbian families) and highlights the importance of children's autonomy within families.

Educational settings are another central place in most children's lives, and scholars, activists and policymakers have identified a variety of ways that teachers, curriculum, school policies, team sports, extracurricular activities and school-based peer cultures shape children's gender and sexuality. The basic question of whether boys and girls receive equitable opportunities to pursue schooling is one that has received much attention internationally, and that question is the first one addressed in Chapter 5. International organizations like the UN have developed programmes to encourage gender equity in education, and many national governments have addressed the issue as well.

Along with progress and initiatives in support of educational opportunities for both boys and girls, the literature reviewed in that chapter reveals controversies, tensions and complex intersections among gender, religion, social class, ability/disability, ethnicity and a host of other factors. Connell, introduced in Chapter 2, argues in a 2010 essay that the international *Education for All* initiative (discussed in Chapter 5) offers some promise, but is also highly problematic in that it simplifies gender to a binary contrast between boys and girls, focuses on school enrolment numbers rather than the content of curriculum and treats boys as the baseline rather than carefully assessing their experiences in school. Both school enrolment statistics and the more nuanced questions of curriculum, teacher expectations and peer interactions are explored in Chapter 5, with examples from around the world. Chen and Rao (2011), for instance, document gendering practices among Chinese kindergarten teachers, concluding: 'Teachers interacted with boys significantly more than girls. They also subtly conveyed traditional Chinese gender values through their repeated use of gendered routines in the kindergartens and their behaviors reflected gender stereotypes' (103). Research results from other age groups and other nations are reviewed in Chapter 5, to illuminate how school settings are implicated in the social construction of childhood gender and sexuality.

In keeping with the literature's emphasis on not just gender but sexuality, and on children's agency, another topic addressed is student activism in relation to gender and sexuality. Gay–straight alliances (GSAs) in secondary schools are one example of youth agency in resisting traditional gender and sexuality expectations in educational settings, and the work of scholars and advocates interested in GSAs is presented in both Chapters 5 and 7. But even GSAs raise complex questions about the balance between youth autonomy and adult control. MacIntosh (2007) applauds the student agency represented in GSAs, but also expresses concern about whether leaving this work to students alone limits the possibilities for deeper institutional change within schools, letting adults bypass their responsibility for ensuring equitable school environments.

> Too often . . . GSAs, and the youth who run them, are viewed absent the complexities under which student power, choice and agency function. The success of GSAs in addressing homophobia is a cause celebre that generates a dangerous either/or dichotomy wherein student action is viewed within an all or nothing system- a system in which, I argue, students who are valuable contributors to change often come to bear the full weight of homophobia education. (131–2)

How GSAs approach the intersections between gender/sexuality and other forms of inequality has been the source of debate and tension as well. For example, do non-heterosexual students face different obstacles if they are from subordinated racial or class groups within their societies? This question is addressed by Johnson (2007).

Example of research: School-based student activism and sexuality

Johnson (2007) discusses the legacy of the first US school-based gay youth group founded in 1972 at New York City's George Washington High School. The founders were primarily students of colour, who sought to create an environment of safety and tolerance in their school and used rights rhetoric to connect their efforts to the larger Gay Liberation movement. '[W]e as gay students demand the same rights (social and political) as "straight" students' (384). While this first school-based gay youth group was founded in a major city, students from a suburban private school are more commonly recognized for having started the first such group. Johnson explores an explanation for the invisibility of the George Washington High School students' efforts in the Gay Liberation Movement, arguing it reflects the movement's tendency to ignore urban youth of colour. 'Racism, classism, and ageism continue to keep the LGBT community unable to represent and honor all of its members, including some of its very first activists' (385).

Reflections on the research

As noted previously, to focus on intersections involves recognizing the ways in which people's experiences are shaped by their location at the intersection of many different identities and inequalities. So, for example, the LGBT students of colour in a lower-income urban high school may be even less visible than their peers with greater economic resources at a private high school, as well as less visible than adult LGBT activists.

Activity

Ask people you know whether their school had a GSA. Once you find someone who says yes, ask them what they remember about the students who were involved in terms of their racial, class, gender and sexual orientation identities. Compare what they tell you to what Johnson argues about the way the George Washington High School students' legacies were shaped not just by their sexual orientation, but by the intersection of their sexual orientation with other important features of their social identities.

Along with families and schools, mass media like television, films, music, books, computer games and internet content constitute another important influence singled out by scholars and children's advocates. Chapter 6 presents research studies and activist interventions related to gender, sexuality and children's media. One consistent pattern across the scholarly literature is that despite progress in media texts for children becoming more gender equitable, significant gender inequalities remain.

Example of research: Gendered images in magazines for Korean girls

Nam, Lee and Hwang (2011) conducted a content analysis of advertising images in the three most popular magazines for adolescent girls in Korea, comparing representations of Korean and Western models. A few quotes summarize their approach and findings:

- *Research question*: 'What are the prevalence and nature of gender stereotypical portrayals in Korean fashion magazines targeting adolescent girls, and how do these portrayals vary as a function of models' race and gender?' (227)
- *Advertisements analysed*: 'We selected 60 advertisements at random from a randomly selected issue (month) of each magazine title per each season resulting in a total of 720 ads from the three magazines' (227).
- *Findings*: 'Korean women were portrayed more often as smaller and shorter than the opposite gender, smiling, pouting, and with a childlike or cute expression than other groups . . . Western women were more female-stereotypically portrayed with their mouth open and in revealing clothes or nudity than any other group . . . while in general all women were stereotypically portrayed, the particular stereotypes associated with women from each race were distinctively different' (234).
- *Implications*: 'Although the current study could not determine which gender images are more likely to be modeled by Korean adolescent girls, it is reasonable to infer that they are prone to emulate what they perceive to be accepted or ideal female roles portrayed by Korean women' (234–5).

Reflections on the research

This research study offers an important reminder that gender patterns in media images can further vary by race, ethnicity, nationality and other intersecting identities. The question is not just how might depictions of males or females reinforce or work against gender stereotypes, but how might those depictions relate to stereotypes of particular racial/ethnic groups as well.

Activity

Locate a magazine aimed at children or adolescents that is read in your country, and flip through the advertisements for pictures that include people. Do you notice any patterns related to gender, and if so, do they seem to vary by ethnicity? What messages about gender or sexuality, and their intersections with ethnicity, do you think any patterns you noticed might convey to young readers?

Nam, Lee and Hwang (2011) recognize the importance of the intersections between gender and ethnicity. In their admission that they can only infer the effects the images they analyse may have on young readers, they also recognize another important theme in the scholarly literature on mass media. Media texts or images do not simply shape readers or viewers in a simple one-way process any more than gender socialization in general can be viewed in simple, one-way terms (see Chapter 2). Media scholars must measure carefully rather than just assume the impact of media, and must acknowledge audience agency – even among children and youth – in how media images are interpreted, refined and resisted. These topics, as well as gender and sexuality-related media activism by and for youth, are therefore addressed as central topics in Chapter 6.

As these introductory examples reveal, family, education and media are three social institutions central to the social construction of gender and sexuality in childhood. Within each domain, many social actors – from parents and relatives, to teachers and school administrators, to media producers and distributors – play key roles. They sometimes reinforce and sometimes reshape traditional patterns, in ways that vary by nation, economic resources, racial/ethnic background and a variety of other factors. Those patterns and variations are detailed in Chapters 4–6.

What role do children themselves play in constructing childhood gender and sexuality?

The three social institutions highlighted so far are generally adult-led forces within which children navigate. But they also execute their own agency and autonomy within each of these arenas, and the importance of that agency is featured more explicitly in Chapter 7's focus on children's peer cultures. Within their families and schools, in city parks and neighbourhoods, as citizens and consumers, children actively develop peer cultures through which they reproduce but also resist and refine traditional expectations around gender and sexuality.

Example of research: Heteronormativity and girls' peer cultures

Myers and Raymond (2010) focus on how heterosexuality is constructed and negotiated in children's peer cultures among young girls, nine years old and under. They use focus group interviews to explore the way these girls are active in 'co-constructing heterosexual ideals' (168). As they talked to their study participants about media, they quickly found that the girls 'redirected the conversation to discuss heterosexual crushes, sex, and dating', a pattern that leads the authors to conclude: 'Girls as young as the first grade proclaimed themselves "boy crazy"' and thus 'worked together to define girls' interests as boy centered' (174). The focus group method, in which they interviewed these young girls in groups of about five to ten, allowed the authors to watch the girls interacting with each other, strengthening their ability to conclude that the girls were influencing each other to adopt and embrace a heterosexual framing and express heterosexual interests. They concluded that the girls 'learned that to be an "appropriate" girl, they should perform heteronormativity for other girls' and '[i]n so doing, they reinforced the gender binary in which girls are measured – and measure themselves – by their relationship to boys' (185).

Reflections on the research

Activity 1

Myers and Raymond argue that the 'boy centeredness' that emerged in their focus group data is a product not of some natural interest these young girls each happened to develop individually, but rather a product of their group interactions within their peer culture. Think about how you might design a research study to tease out the interactional-level process that produces this kind of self-definition among young girls, in order to explore how peer cultures establish or magnify pressures towards heteronormativity.

Activity 2

In their article, Myers and Raymond do not report on whether or how they shared the results of their research with the girls who participated or with their parents or teachers. If you conducted the kind of study you designed in Activity 1, do you think it would be important to share the results with the participants? And if so, what effect do you think would be appropriate for you, as an adult researcher, to try to have on the girls' autonomous peer culture?

A focus on children's peer cultures and on interactional-level construction of gender and sexuality are both consistent with trends in the literatures on childhood and gender. Chapter 7, as the last of the four chapters exploring key sites at which gender and sexuality are shaped in childhood, highlights the active role of children as interpretive reproducers (see Chapter 1). Along with many examples of the ways in which peer cultures enforce traditional boundaries for gender and sexuality, the chapter also addresses resistance, both in everyday peer cultures and in more formal participation by youth in organizations and movements that seek social change. But even while fore-grounding youth agency, the literature reviewed in this chapter also high-lights the important limits imposed by adults, in terms of the constraints youth face from both informal and formal adult power.

What role does the state play in constructing gender and sexuality in childhood?

One form of adult power recognized by researchers and advocates is the role of the state, in terms of public policy, legal decisions in the courts, the availability of government funding and other specific examples. As childhood gender and sexuality are shaped and refined in families, schools, the media and children's peer cultures, national and local government policies provide context and constraint. Given that the influence of the state weaves its way throughout the other specific arenas addressed in this book, it is considered as relevant within each of the subsequent chapters rather than being featured in its own chapter.

Key points: The state and children's gender and sexuality, select examples

A brief preview of some of the particular examples of the role of the state that are addressed in forthcoming chapters offers a clear sense of its importance in the social construction of gender and sexuality in childhood.

- *Courts and law*: The role of the courts in approving parental requests to seek medical treatment for intersex and transgender children and adolescents (Chapter 4); the legal rights of 'sexual minority' youth internationally (Chapter 4); court decisions related to Muslim girls' attire at school (Chapter 5); state regulations restricting youth access to sexually explicit media (Chapter 6).
- *Public policy*: Government outreach efforts designed to enhance youth sexual and reproductive health (Chapter 4); government policies to provide equitable public edu-cation for girls and boys (Chapter 5); state policy in relation to non-heterosexual and non-gender-normative students in schools (Chapter 5); quality and design of public playgrounds in terms of implications for gendered peer cultures (Chapter 7).
- *Government funding*: the impact of government funding for educational facilities in terms of their implications for gender equity (Chapter 5); government and interna-tional/intergovernmental funding of media advocacy initiatives for youth (Chapter 6); dependence on state funding as a constraint on youth agency in formal organizations (Chapter 7).

From social institutions such as the family, education and mass media to the active role that children themselves play, and cross-cut by the influence of the state and variations by intersecting inequalities, childhood gender and sexuality are socially constructed by a wide range of actors and influences in a complex process of stability and change. The remaining chapters of this book lay out current scholarship on that process from many different academic disciplines, with a consistent emphasis on children's agency, autonomy and voice, as well as the diversity of childhoods both within and between the many nations of the world. Advocacy and activism receive consistent attention too, as interventions at the level of everyday interaction to the level of international NGOs help shape and reshape gender and sexuality in childhood.

Chapter activities

Activity 1: Connections across various influences

Though the remainder of this book is organized into chapters focused on family, education, media and children's peer cultures, you will notice frequent overlaps between these various sites. Families and schools intersect, children's peer cultures play out in households and schoolyards, and so on. Looking back over the various research findings previewed in this chapter, pick out at least one example of children's gender and sexuality being shaped by not just one of these influences but by two or more at once.

Activity 2: Organized movements for social change

When we view gender and childhood as social constructs, variable across geographic locations, diverse subgroups and historical periods, the potential for social change is immediately apparent. Organized movements for social change are emphasized throughout this book. As a starting point for thinking about social change in relation to gender and sexuality, select any one of the following websites and explore it briefly. Take some notes on the issues and initiatives addressed by the organization you selected, and think about those in relation to the topics explored in this book. Do you see evidence of some of the themes and debates highlighted so far?

- **Gender Identity Research and Education Society** (gires.org.uk): UK-based organization advocating for transgender individuals and their families, including focus on youth issues.
- **Groundspark** (groundspark.org/our-films-and-campaigns/straightlaced): US-based organization that promotes social change through film; one of their featured projects is the film *Straightlaced: How gender's got us all tied up*, which addresses how youth are affected by gender expectations.
- **UNICEF** (unicef.org/gender): International United Nations Children's Fund, whose programs and initiatives include many focused on gender.

Summary

This chapter has:

- Introduced the specific topics covered in subsequent chapters: family, education, mass media and children's peer cultures;
- Highlighted the importance of the state in shaping gender and sexuality in childhood, both as a force that can constrain but also help shift traditional patterns and inequalities;
- Presented a series of examples of research, one from each of the topics addressed in Chapters 4–7, as a preview of the kinds of research findings explored in detail throughout the remainder of the book;
- Emphasized social change as a key theme through a chapter activity focused on formal organizing to address gender inequalities affecting children and youth.

Further reading

Bajaj, M. (2009), 'Un/doing gender?: A case study of school policy and practice in Zambia', *International Review of Education*, 55, 5/6, 483–502.

Case study evaluating the effectiveness of policy in a private Zambian secondary school. The author finds that 'pedagogical practices deployed by this school have generally succeeded in destabilizing norms of gender subordination and gender-based violence' (483).

Seaman, A. and DeJean, W. (2010), 'Editorial', *Australasian Journal of Early Childhood*, 35, 1, i–iii.

Editors' introduction to a special issue which 'brings together authors from Australia, New Zealand and the United States to help highlight the topic of sexuality in early childhood through multiple voices and international understandings' (ii).

Wallien, M., Veenstra, R., Kreukels, B. and Cohen-Kettenis, P. (2010), 'Peer group status of gender dysphoric children', *Archives of Sexual Behavior*, 39, 2, 553–60.

Quantitative analysis of peer bullying experienced by children with significantly gender-nonconforming behaviour patterns in the Netherlands. Authors conclude that gender non-conforming boys are especially rejected by their same-sex peers.

Research details

Styles of toy play with sons and daughters

Peer-reviewed journal. Researchers Wood, Desmarais and Gugula (2002) recruited 48 boys and girls between the ages of 24 and 72 months, as well as

144 adult men and women to participate in their experimental play sessions. Along with observation of the play sessions, the study included a questionnaire about the appropriateness of various toys administered to the adults after the play session.

School-based student activism and sexuality

Peer-reviewed journal. Johnson (2007) analyses how student involvement in the Gay Rights Movement has been documented. She relies on historical documents – pamphlets, articles and other existing histories – as well as scholarly work on the topic.

Gendered images in magazines for Korean girls

Peer-reviewed journal. Nam, Lee and Hwang (2011) selected the three Korean magazines aimed at an adolescent readership that charged the highest advertising prices (which they treat as a measure of how popular the magazine is). For the two-year period of 2002–3, they coded 720 randomly selected full-page ads that included at least one person, coding seven specific aspects of the characteristics of the one or two most prominent people in the ad.

Heteronormativity and girls' peer cultures

Peer reviewed journal. Myers and Raymond (2010) gathered their data in the United States, at a single primary school in a 'rural, primarily white community' (171). This article is based on the focus group data in which they organized 43 girls into a series of age-based focus groups. Sessions averaged 75 minutes, and the researchers took detailed notes on each group.

Part 3
Implications for Children's Lives

Gender, Sexuality and the Family

Introduction and key questions

As a site crucially important in the lives of children and adults, the family is of interest to scholars in many fields. This chapter explores how children's gender and sexuality are reproduced, refined and resisted within families, with particular attention to parents but also to the many influences that surround them, and their children. Children's autonomy is emphasized as well because children are not only shaped by families but are active agents within those families too. All of this is organized within a series of key questions:

- How do parents shape children's gender and sexuality?
- Who influences parents and families as they think about childhood gender and sexuality?
- What other aspects of families impact children's gender and sexuality?
- What about gender- and sexuality-related autonomy and agency for children within families?

How do parents shape children's gender and sexuality?

From the moment of birth and even before, parents begin shaping their children's gender and sexuality. In a classic 1974 study, Luria, Provenzano and Rubin found that US parents described their newborns' physical and character traits differently depending on whether they were boys or girls, even when those infants were similar physically and behaviourally. Perceiving their infants differently by gender in the absence of actual differences is significant, of course, because of the potential for a self-fulfilling prophecy as parents treat their babies based on those perceptions. For example, Fine (2010) reports on experimental studies documenting that parents who were asked to set an incline ramp to a challenging level for their crawling infant tended to set it higher for sons than daughters. Likely viewing their sons as more physically capable, they challenge them in a way that may actually produce that capability rather than reflecting it. Clearfield and Nelson (2006) also use evidence from lab experiments to reveal differences in how mothers of six- to fourteen-month old children treat daughters and sons. Mothers tend to engage in more conversation and direct interaction with daughters, while offering more instructions and less interaction to sons. In the process, they may encourage daughters to develop stronger communication and interpersonal skills while encouraging sons to develop greater technical and problem-solving skills as well as enhanced independence. Another important kind of differential treatment by parents involves the allocation of family resources and family obligations to sons and daughters. Though relevant in all societies, one example of the role of parents in shaping children's opportunities by gender comes from Croll's (2006) critique of aid programmes in southeast Asia.

In children's programmes, there is still the assumption that the family is a benign institution operating in the best interests of the child with fair and equal allocation of resources to all children. However, recent research suggests that it is not so much the availability of services for education and health that are of import, but parental attitudes, behaviour and choices affecting familial resource allocation to food, health care and education. (1291)

Croll argues that failing to differentiate children by gender in the targets of development programmes leaves it to parents to allocate aid resources within a family unit, which they often do in ways that disadvantage girls. Differential treatment by parents and guardians is also addressed in Jacquemin's (2006) research on young girls working as domestic labourers in the Ivory Coast. She finds that relatives sometimes arrange employment situations in other people's homes for these girls not on the basis of economic necessity for the family as a unit but in order to benefit themselves individually at the child's expense, a pattern she argues is enabled when development programmes assume economic exploitation is only likely to occur outside the family. Both of these examples point to the potential for differential treatment by parents that disadvantages girls, but also to the need to recognize cultural variations in the implementation of development programmes. In a research study on gender and education in rural Niger that is considered in Chapter 5, Greany (2008) argues that Western-inspired development programmes should be sensitive to local contexts and cultural gender norms even as they engage in activism aimed at increasing opportunities for girls. The same caution is perhaps merited in relation to Croll's (2006) and Jacquemin's (2006) conclusions, as they are European-based scholars investigating gendered practices in other regions of the world.

From early ages, through childhood and adolescence and even potentially before birth, differential treatment by parents is detailed in a vast literature from around the world (see Table 4.1). The potential impact of such treatment must be considered in the context of children's agency and autonomy, with attention to children's ability to resist and refine the expectations directed at them. But given the role parents play in shaping children's lives, it is crucial to consider their power as well.

Table 4.1 Selected research findings on parental treatment of sons and daughters

Author(s)	Location of research, age range of children and research method	Parental treatment documented	Potential impact on children
Kane (2009)	USA 3–5 year olds Interviews with parents	When asked about any preferences they held for having sons versus daughters before they became parents, interviewees expressed highly traditional images of what a boy versus girl would act like and enjoy	Parental anticipation of sons versus daughters may create a self-fulfilling prophecy, in which parents eventually provide the opportunities that craft the very interests and tendencies they assumed those children would have
Martin and Luke (2010)	USA 3–6 year olds Survey of mothers	Mothers talk more to daughters about romance, reproduction and morality of sexual relationships; they do not tend to talk about sexual pleasure to either sons or daughters	Cultural 'double standard' in which female sexuality is discouraged; girls' heteronormative orientation to romance encouraged; for both boys and girls, a tendency to view sex as an arena of risk rather than pleasure
Raley and Bianchi (2006)	Various nations Various age ranges Critical synthesis of existing research	Parents assign more hours of housework chores, as well as more typically female chores, to daughters	Girls develop skills in traditionally female domestic chores and may view them as their obligation; girls have less time available for other pursuits than their brothers
Bos and Sandfort (2010)	Netherlands 8–12 year olds Survey	Sons reported more parental pressure to conform to gender expectations than daughters	Boys encouraged to develop typically masculine characteristics and interests while girls may develop a greater range of characteristics and interests
Chu, Tsay and Yu (2008)	Taiwan Various ages Survey of adults	More years of formal schooling offered to sons than daughters, particularly if parents grew up in families with such differential treatment	Greater education and more occupational and social opportunities available to boys and men
Chaudhuri and Roy (2009)	India Primary and middle school children Survey of adults	Parents with less formal education are especially likely to have sons who complete more formal schooling than their daughters	Greater education and more occupational and social opportunities made available to boys and men

Author(s)	Location of research, age range of children and research method	Parental treatment documented	Potential impact on children
Choi and Lee (2006)	India Pre-birth and early childhood Survey of parents' health behaviours	Among rural populations, mothers seek greater early childhood immunization for sons rather than daughters	Higher quality health care and better health outcomes for boys than girls
Vekiri and Chronaki (2008)	Greece 10–11 year olds Survey	Boys reported more parental support for computer use than girls	Greater reported self-efficacy in terms of computer skills for boys
Dilorio, Pluhar and Belcher (2003)	USA Adolescents Critical synthesis of existing research	Mothers report more communication about sex and sexuality with daughters than with sons	Adolescent girls may end up with more knowledge of risks and more adult support in their sexual decision-making than adolescent boys
Dwairy and colleagues (2006)	Algeria, Egypt, Israel, Jordan, Lebanon, Palestine, Saudi Arabia and Yemen Adolescents Survey	Adolescent girls reported more authoritative behaviours by their parents (direction coupled with explanation and discussion) while boys reported more authoritarian behaviour (strict rules without discussion or negotiation)	Adolescent girls may tend to identify more closely with their parents' traditional values, while boys may experience more conflict with parents due to stricter discipline

Example of research: Differential discipline for sons

During extended fieldwork in rural Vietnam, Rydstrøm (2006) observed parents' and grandparents' interactions with boys and girls, and documents the harsh physical discipline that some fathers and grandfathers use with boys. She considers this physical punishment in the context of the United Nations Convention on the Rights of the Child, which prohibits it, but also in the context of traditional norms of male power in Vietnamese society. She argues that deeply held notions of the honour due to older men shape how fathers and grandfathers react to boys who do not show respect and obedience to their male elders: 'they do not accept such opposition from a (male) youngster. The men lose patience, fly into a rage and end up using physical punishment' (343). In the process, they construct a particular notion of masculinity for boys, one that positions 'men as superior and powerful' but also as emotionally 'hot' and prone to violence. Through this kind of discipline and the form of masculinity it valorizes, Rydstrøm argues that a 'cycle of violence can be passed on from one generation to the next' (343).

Reflections on the research

As a Swedish researcher studying Vietnam, Rydstrøm's criticism of Vietnamese customs might imply that violence against children is not an issue in more developed Western settings. Unfortunately, violence against children is evident throughout the world.

Example of research – Cont'd

Activity

Search the internet to learn more about corporal punishment laws and rates of violence against children within families in your own country. Activism aimed at reducing corporal punishment is also evident worldwide. For an example from Vietnam, check out the corporal punishment project of the Centre for Studies and Applied Sciences in Gender, Family, Women and Adolescents (CSAGA at www.csaga.org.vn/) in Hanoi. Then see if you can find some similar project in your own nation by searching online. How does comparing Vietnam to your country help you think about the complexities of defining abuse according to the UNCRC while also recognizing the unique context of each culture?

Parents also play a part in their children's developing sexuality, through the education and information they offer or fail to offer about sexual activity and sexual health and in the support or acknowledgement they offer for non-heterosexual orientations. In the latter realm, D'Augelli, Grossman, Starks and Sinclair (2010) conducted interviews with gay, lesbian and bisexual adolescents, and document that their internalized homophobia tended to decline after they revealed their sexual orientation to their parents. While some parents were specifically supportive, even when that was not the case the mere act of parental acknowledgement seems to be associated with greater self-acceptance for these young people.

Who influences parents and families as they think about childhood gender and sexuality?

As Rydstrøm's (2006) research highlights, parents do not act in a vacuum. The fathers and grandfathers she observed in rural Vietnam are influenced by social customs in their local areas, and all parents are similarly surrounded by many social, cultural and political forces as they think about their children's gender and sexuality.

Example of research: Judgements by others in everyday social interaction

In my own research (Kane 2006), I have explored how parents think about gendering their 3- to 5-year-old children in the USA. My interviews with 42 parents of children in this age range turned up many references to worries about how they or their children would be judged by others if they failed to live up to the gender expectations that surround them. Following other scholars in gender studies and symbolic interactionist sociology, I refer to this social pressure as 'accountability', the way in which we are all accountable to social assessment by others in the everyday interactions of our lives (see Chapter 2 for more on interactional-level social construction of gender). In my study, accountability to others was especially and frequently mentioned as a reason for encouraging young children to follow gendered rules when:

- The child in question is a boy, reflecting the greater social pressure for gender conformity placed on boys;
- The parent in question is a heterosexual mother, reflecting a general tendency these women felt to protect their sons from rejection by peers but also a particular concern about pressure from their children's fathers, who they say tend to judge gender nonconformity by boys harshly;
- Or the parent is gay or lesbian, reflecting the additional judgement these parents feel flows from a homophobic society; as one lesbian parent put it 'I feel held up to the world to make sure that his masculinity is in check' (169).

Reflections on the research

Activity
My research focuses on the idea of accountability, which I define as 'the way in which we are all accountable to social assessment by others'. In the three bulleted examples above, to what social pressures or assessments are parents accountable? And how might accountability affect:

- Parents of intersex children,
- Parents of gay or lesbian children,
- A single father raising daughters?

The process through which parents account for the gender of their children is particularly complex in cases where a child's gender identity or behaviours fall outside what is considered typical in their cultural context. Meadow (2011, 742) conducted an extensive ethnographic study of families in which a child is transgender ('children whose gender identity does not conform to the gender category they were assigned at birth') or gender-variant ('children whose gender presentation may appear deviant to an outside observer, but whose internal sense of self is aligned with their assigned gender category'). As she points out, parents play at least two roles in this process: 'they are, at moments, the ones demanding explanations of their children, yet they are also the proxy voices permitted (and often required) to make declarative statements in the medical and social environments their children inhabit' (730). This is especially striking for the parents in her research study, because 'their children radically transgress social expectations for boys and girls, pushing their parents, teachers and larger societal institutions to challenge the fundamental notion of a dichotomous gender system' (731). Meadow (2011) profiles families who have 'chosen to affirm their child's gender complexity' (731), a reminder that despite many constraints, children and their parents also execute agency in relation to childhood gender and sexuality: 'these families are part of a larger push to re-articulate the rules by which we live in our minds, bodies, and souls' (742).

Meadow's research highlights the role of medical authorities in the lives of the parents she studied. A few brief examples highlight additional research on the role of medical as well as religious authorities.

- Ahmed, Morrison and Hughes (2004) argue that ambiguously sexed infants should be assigned a socially accepted gender category as soon as possible, warning parents and health care practitioners that placing a child outside the two socially recognized gender categories 'is not a feasible option considering that in most cultures around the world, gender variants are not treated as equals' (849) (see Chapter 2 for more about this article).
- Garcia, Gray-Stanley and Ramirez-Valles (2008) interview Latino young adult men in the United States who identify as gay, bisexual or transgender about their religious experiences, and find that some of their interviewees report Catholic religious teachings as a factor in their parents' strong disapproval of their emerging sexual/ gender identities in adolescence.
- Robson's (2004) fieldwork in rural Nigeria documents how Muslim mothers' seclusion among the Hausa requires them to send their children out to complete work beyond domestic spaces. This religious and cultural practice of adult women's domestic seclusion provides an opportunity for children to become 'competent agents making significant economic contributions' (193), allowing not just sons but also daughters to develop skills in economic exchange.

State and NGO policies can also direct parents' options, shaping how they think about or can respond to various gender and sexuality-related outcomes with or for their children.

- Beh and Diamond (2005) analyse family court decisions in Australia related to medical treatment for intersex and transgender children/adolescents, highlighting cases in which parents and children who wished to seek treatment needed first to obtain the approval of the courts.
- Hicks (2008) criticizes the way social work evaluations conducted during the adoption and foster care process in the United Kingdom have questioned the ability of

gay and lesbian applicants to provide proper gender socialization to children, suggesting strong pressure for such applicants to engage in traditional gendering of any children eventually placed in their care.

- Croll (2006) praises a pamphlet put out by the Council for the Welfare of Children of the Philippine government, entitled 'Girls Have Rights Too'; according to Croll, this simple, reader-friendly pamphlet encourages various social actors – including parents – to understand better 'the ways in which Filipino culture binds girls to gender stereotypes and fosters acceptance of exploitative practices' (1294) and thus represents an effort by state policy to promote greater gender equality for children.

Example of research: Public policy shaping sexuality-related parenting practices

The title of a research study by public health researcher/advocates Baptiste and six colleagues (2009) summarizes nicely their purpose: 'Increasing Parental Involvement in Youth HIV Prevention: A Randomized Caribbean Study'. Working in Trinidad and Tobago, the authors note strong support from the Prime Minister's office. With increasing rates of youth HIV infection and low rates of condom use among sexually active male youth, the authors and other public health professionals in Trinidad and Tobago hope to see parents get more involved in communicating information and monitoring activity among their adolescent children. To encourage and test that outcome, they designed the 'Trinidad and Tobago Family HIV Workshop', which promotes 'effective parenting as a 'protective shield' around youth that buffers them against personal, social, and cultural sexual pressures' (497).

The researchers identified parents of 12- to 14-year-old children, randomly assigning the parents *and* their children together to either a control group that completed a general workshop or an intervention group that received the more intensive, targeted 'Family HIV Workshop'. Using pre-test and post-test questionnaires, the authors (2009, 495) conclude that the intervention had the following positive effects:

- Increased parental knowledge regarding HIV;
- Increased general communication with adolescents;
- Increased conversations about sex with adolescents, including conversations about sexual risks and sexual values;
- Increased monitoring of adolescents.

On the basis of these changes, the authors argue that the workshop intervention is an effective way to increase parental involvement in youth HIV prevention efforts.

Reflections on the research

Activity

How does this study reveal the role that research can play in activism? And what do you think about the way the workshop described in the study involves an active role for both parents and youth?

Another source of influence is the parenting experts who fill volumes of books with gender and sexuality-related advice that some parents seek. Along with Riggs (2008), discussed in Chapter 2, here are two more samples of the kind of gender and sexuality-related messages researchers have identified in parenting advice books.

- Krafchick, Zimmerman, Haddock and Banning (2005) conduct a content analysis of bestselling parenting books in the United States, concluding that over 80 per cent of the implicit gendered messages in the books are traditional/stereotypical; these messages reproduce assumptions that mothers should be primary caregivers to children, boys are naturally more independent and girls are naturally more nurturing.
- Martin, Hutson, Kazyak and Scherrer (2010) review 29 parenting advice books sold in the United States that address gay and lesbian children. They conclude that these books offer parents three strategies in responding to their children's non-heterosexual orientation, all of which imply that orientation is somehow problematic: 'relying on professionals for overcoming the grief of having a gay or lesbian child, normalizing gay and lesbian identity, and using "good" parenting skills' to continue to love their children unconditionally (960).

Influenced by a diverse array of religions and cultures, as well as by expert advice, public policy and everyday accountability to others in interaction, parental approaches may be situated in the family, but they are part of a much broader process of the social construction of gender and sexuality in childhood. That process includes active agency on the part of the children as well, a point that receives more explicit attention in the final section of this chapter.

Example of research: The intersection of race, gender and expert advice as parents navigate gender reaffirmation

US researcher McGuffey (2008) interviewed parents whose sons were participants in a group therapy program for sexually abused boys. McGuffey's participants were parents of sons who had been abused by other relatives, neighbours, family friends or babysitters, usually men. In an approach that attends to the role of race and class in shaping gender and sexual identities, he argues that parents often respond to the sexual abuse of their sons by engaging in a process of 'gender reaffirmation'.

- Worried that same-sex sexual abuse might shape their son's eventual sexual orientation, many parents sought to bolster their son's masculinity and heterosexuality despite the therapy programme's emphasis on gender and sexuality as fluid and all forms of gender and sexual identity as worthy of validation.

- McGuffey views the kind of hyper-masculine behaviour that has been identified among some sexually abused boys as shaped at least partly by parents: 'it is the parents in this study who push and encourage their sons' participation into hegemonic forms of masculinity out of their desire for heterosexual boys' (235).
- That hegemonic, or culturally validated, form of masculinity involves 'sports, the objectification of girls and women, emotional detachment, and homophobia' (235).

McGuffey finds this pattern particularly notable among non-white families, as the trauma of same-sex sexual abuse 'heighten(s) anxiety over racial subordination that increases their investment in traditional gender reaffirmation' (217). In other words, though generally of comfortable economic status given the cost of the therapy programme, the non-white families participating face the additional burdens of racial inequality in the United States, burdens that may make establishing a socially validated masculinity for their sons feel all the more important to them.

Reflections on the research

Activity
How do race and gender intersect in shaping the accountability pressures that the parents in McGuffey's study seem to feel? How do you think those pressures might differ if the parents were less economically secure?

What other aspects of families impact children's gender and sexuality?

So far the focus of this chapter has been on parents' direct treatment of children and the forces that influence those parents from outside the family. But it is also important to explore other influences within the family that might impact children's gender and sexuality.

Researchers have explored the ways in which indirect gendering may occur as children model the gendered behaviours and divisions of labour they notice among their parents. For example, Cunningham (2001) analyses US survey data revealing that adult men are more likely to participate in household chores if their fathers did so when they were young, and adult women less likely to carry the burden of housework if their mothers worked outside the home when they were young. van Putten, Dykstra and Schippers (2008) use Dutch survey data to show that adult women tend to work longer hours in paid employment if their mothers worked longer hours during their childhood. A more disturbing pattern is evident in a study by Phillips and Phillips (2010). Focused particularly on trying to improve the quality of services provided to children exposed to family violence, they argue that US researchers have over-emphasized statistical approaches that fail to understand the phenomenon from the child's perspective. They advocate instead for the kind of 'ethnographic approach' that 'emerges in UK- and Australia-based research with children exposed to DV (domestic violence)', an approach they consider more 'child-centered' (294). Using this approach, they find that exposure to domestic violence often leads children to more deeply gendered identities, as they attempt to make themselves 'normal' by acting out gender stereotypes. While the counsellors in the particular program Phillips and Phillips studied encourage the children to reject conventional gender stereotypes as a source of the violence they observed between aggressive fathers and more passive mothers, the children themselves resist because their exposure to violence has left them feeling marked outside the mainstream. Phillips and Phillips advocate for practitioners to understand more fully how some of these children need the social safety of conforming to gender expectations. They also offer another example of an indirect path through which parents' gendered behaviours can shape children's gendered development. Along with patterns like these, however, some studies show a lack of association between gendered role modelling and outcomes for children, indicating that indirect effects occur sometimes but not consistently. For example, in a large-scale survey of UK families, Stevens, Golombok and Beveridge (2002) document that 3-year-old children show similar patterns of gendered activities and behaviours regardless of whether they are raised in single-mother households or two-parent heterosexual households.

The question of whether and how gay and lesbian households offer a particular context that shapes children's gender and sexuality has been of interest to researchers, policymakers and advocates. A few examples of how people have explored this question sketch an outline of the potential impact of another kind of household structure.

- Stacey and Biblarz (2001) conduct a comprehensive review of existing literature, and argue that children raised in gay and lesbian households tend to have more flexible gender-role enactment and less rigid approaches to sexuality.
- Bos and Sandfort (2010) administered survey questionnaires to Dutch children aged 8 to 12 living in heterosexual and gay/lesbian households. They reach a similar conclusion to Stacey and Biblarz: 'Children in lesbian families felt less parental pressure to conform to gender stereotypes, were less likely to experience their own gender as superior and were more likely to be uncertain about future heterosexual romantic involvement' (114).

- In articles whose titles capture their arguments succinctly, several UK psychologists assert that the lack of different-sex role models in gay or lesbian households has no negative impact on children's gender-role development and thus should not be considered problematic in public policy debates: Clarke and Kitzinger's (2005) '"We're not living on planet lesbian": Constructions of male role models in debates about lesbian families' and Hicks' (2008) 'Gender role models: Who needs 'em?!'
- In an international review, Švab (2007) notes that gay and lesbian parents face particularly strong criticism of their ability to raise appropriately gendered children in countries such as Slovenia, which have 'even higher levels of homophobia and social distance' (53).

Example of research: The voices of children from lesbian families

Lubbe (2008) explores the experiences of eight children in lesbian families in South Africa, a particularly interesting national context given nearly two decades of legal decisions that have significantly expanded the family rights of gay, lesbian, bisexual and transgendered people. In the author's own words, key aspects of the study are as follows:

- 'My interest for investigating lesbian-headed families is to explore what happens to children of lesbian parents when they move from their homes into the world and how they negotiate the possible difficulties inherent in inviting the world (in the form of close friends, classmates, peers, other significant adults) into their family homes' (327).
- 'I chose narrative inquiry (a series of in-depth weekly interviews) because it attempts to understand and represent experiences through the stories that individuals live and tell' (328).
- 'The findings revealed that a common denominator among all eight children was that they were acutely aware of the propensity of people to react in diverse ways to the notion of lesbian-headed (households) and the idea of such couples raising children. This awareness endowed them with unusual sensitivity that characterizes all their social interactions' (355).

Lubbe documents that the children she interviewed faced stigma and discrimination in some of their social encounters, but also support and acceptance in others, emphasizing social change and children's strength in actively negotiating their social worlds.

Reflections on the research

Activity

Consider Lubbe's research on the children of LGBT families in South Africa, as well as the patterns noted previously regarding gay and lesbian parents in four other nations by Stacy and Biblarz (2001), Bos and Sandfort (2010), Clarke and Kitzinger (2005), Hicks (2008) and Švab (2007). What do you notice about variations by national context in the pressures surrounding parents as they gender their children and what strikes you as similar across these studies?

Along with household structures in terms of the number and sex and employment status of parents, children's gendered paths are also influenced by their siblings. Table 4.2 offers several examples of the variety of ways in which the gender composition of siblings within a family can shape gendered outcomes for children.

Table 4.2 Selected research findings on the impact of siblings on gendered outcomes

Author(s)	Location of research, age range of children and research method	Impact documented
McHale, Crouter and Whiteman (2003)	USA Various ages Critical review of existing research	Children with same-sex older siblings are often more gender-typed, especially among boys; this effect is evident after controlling for parents' degree of gender-typing (in other words, older same-sex siblings tend to exert some influence over and above whatever influence parents have exerted)
Pande (2003)	India Various ages National health survey of adults, focusing on data from rural areas	Sons born to families with multiple older female siblings tend to have the most positive nutrition and immunization outcomes, suggesting that parents are especially likely to invest in boys' health for the first son born after multiple daughters
Karniol (2009)	Israel 5–6 year olds Experiment with children	Kindergarten children with older siblings had more fixed ideas about gender, and this was particularly the case for boys with an older same-sex sibling
Chu, Tsay and Yu (2008)	Taiwan Various ages Survey of adults	Lesser investment of education resources in girls reported in Table 4.1 is more pronounced if they also have older male siblings

The findings in Table 4.2 are an important reminder that not only do parental actions, beliefs and characteristics mark the family context in which children's gender is shaped, but other family members like siblings play a role too. As McHale, Crouter and Whiteman (2003) put it, siblings 'have been relatively neglected in the story of family gender socialization'. They go on to note that the important effects of siblings can be 'direct, as when brothers or sisters serve as role models or social partners, as well as indirect, as when they serve as sources for social comparison, help to shape the structure of their families, and influence everyday family activities and routines' (126).

What about gender- and sexuality-related autonomy and agency for children within families?

Though the focus of this chapter is on how families impact children's gender and sexuality, the exploration of that topic has also included attention to children's agency within families. Given the importance of children's autonomy and rights, this chapter ends with a few more examples. In Chapter 2, Rogers' (2009) argument for respecting the sexual agency of youth with learning disabilities, and thus providing them adequate sexual education in schools, was mentioned. But the larger context of that article involves Rogers' discussion of her own daughter, who has learning disabilities significant enough to warrant education in a school for children with disabilities. Despite the temptation to deny and ignore her daughter's emerging sexual interest out of fear for whether she had the cognitive capacity to make decisions about sexual risks, Rogers also recognizes what she calls her daughter's 'sexual citizenship and rights to a sexual identity'. Striking that balance between protection and autonomy is an act parents must negotiate in the context of intersecting factors such as disability, religion and culture, but Rogers' article is a fascinating example of the dilemmas that arise when a parent takes their child's sexual autonomy and agency seriously. Also relevant to sexuality-related information is a study by Hyde and five colleagues (2010) focused on parent–adolescent communication about sex in Ireland. They argue that a complicating element in parents' attempts to speak openly with their children about sexual activity and sexual risks is those parents' desire to respect their children's autonomy.

> The concern that parents conveyed about their children's sensibilities – for example their eagerness not to embarrass or annoy the young person by insisting on a discussion – appears to be rooted in the shifting power of children historically and the new cultural aspiration of maintaining harmonious and friendly relations with one's children. (366)

A striking case of acknowledging children's agency is offered by Montgomery (2010), whose ethnographic research involving child prostitutes in Thailand focusses attention on the constraints and potential harm of their work with emphasis on their own interpretations of it. While holding their Western adult 'sex tourist' clients responsible for exploiting these children, Montgomery also notes that from their own perspective, 'prostitution was not the worst, or most feared, option open to these children' (180). It paid well, allowing them to help their families with much-needed resources, and was 'less physically demanding' than other options like 'scavenging, working in sweatshops, and begging' (180). As she concludes, with a strong emphasis on children's agency as family members:

> My intention in this article has not been to condone child prostitution but to celebrate these children's resilience and admire their strong sense of obligation to their families and to argue that labelling and analyzing them only as prostitutes, and not also as children, does them a further disservice. (186)

Interview with Heather Montgomery about her research on child prostitution in Thailand

Heather Montgomery is Senior Lecturer in Childhood Studies at the Open University in the United Kingdom and a social anthropologist who focuses on issues of childhood, adolescence, sexuality and children's rights.

Emily Kane:	Thinking back, what surprised you the most about the process or results of your research in Thailand?
Heather Montgomery:	When I first went to Thailand, I wanted to study issues of child labour. I switched to the specific focus on prostitution early on when I realised what a huge topic it had become in the media and among NGOs. However I assumed that most of the 'children' working as prostitutes would in fact be teenagers and between 15 and 18 years old. My hypothesis was that in Thailand, these young women would not be seen as children, they might already have been married, possibly even be mothers themselves. My view was that the Western notion of a child as a person aged under 18 would be untenable in Thailand. What surprised me was how very young the children I ended up working with were, children between the ages of 6 and 12. There was no discussion about whether or not these were children – everyone acknowledged them as such. Despite this however they continued to work as prostitutes.

Emily Kane:	Global variations in gender and sexuality-related issues during childhood form a central focus of this book. Could you comment briefly on what you have learned about such variations and their importance through your research?
Heather Montgomery:	What I learned was that sexual abuse was seen very differently in places such as the slum village where I worked. I would not want to generalize too strongly on the basis of this one village but there seemed a very different attitude to the relationship between sexuality and identity and sexual abuse and identity. There is a strong cultural belief in the West that sexual abuse 'ruins' a child, steals their childhood and damages them fundamentally at a psychic level. In Thailand this belief just wasn't there. Although there was a discourse among local NGOs that children would be irreparably harmed through prostitution, this was largely expressed in physical terms. They tended to claim that children would contract AIDS and die but did not on the whole emphasize psychological damage (although in the Western press this wasn't always the case). Although it is possible to claim that these children were wilfully ignorant, they claimed that being a prostitute was not central to their identity. They focused instead on relationships between themselves and others, positioning themselves as dutiful daughters doing good to the family. All other interpretations were strongly rejected. While sex was a central part of their lives to outsiders and seen as the most interesting thing about them in some ways, it was, for the children themselves, a means to an end. Having said this I do think that discourses about sexual abuse and sexual exploitation are becoming globalized. I certainly saw a change in the 18 months I was there and children were increasingly aware of the stigma against selling sex.

A clear reminder about children's autonomy and agency also comes up in studies that document the potential for children's resistance to gendered messages from their parents. For example, Aghajanian and four colleagues (2007) report on survey data from Iranian high school students, and find that high school girls increasingly prefer non-traditional opportunities regardless of how traditional their own family/community is. Rather than passively absorbing their parents' preferences, these girls actively interpret a broad range of social cues from their surroundings.

Example of research: Sexual identity rights

Chan (2006) offers a detailed analysis of existing laws, conventions and policies related to what he calls 'sexual minority identities' in a global context, with particular attention to UK legal policy. He argues that the UNCRC should be applied to the protection of sexual minority identity rights of youth in the United Kingdom and globally.

> Sexual orientation is a human development occurring primarily prior to or during adolescence. It should therefore be hoped that the United Nations Convention on the Rights of the Child (CRC) – the foremost international instrument vis-a-vis children's rights that all but two states, namely the United States and Somalia, have ratified – would explicitly address the attendant issues and concerns in a legally binding framework. Unfortunately, the CRC fails to mention sexual orientation in its entire text (162).

He considers this failure troubling, but also asserts that it does not prevent the CRC from being applied to protect such rights. He goes on to argue in detail, using previous research studies, theories of adolescent development and a thorough review of legal decisions from around the world, that Article 8 of the UNCRC, the section that addresses the child's right to identity, should be applied to sexual minority identities of youth so that their autonomy and rights are respected fully. Regardless of what their parents or others around them may believe, Chan emphasizes the adolescent's rights.

Reflections on the research

The rights of 'sexual minorities' in general, and of 'sexual minority youth' in particular, are controversial, with some religions and nations more open to a variety of sexual identities than others.

Activity

How would more attention to 'sexual minority identities' in national and international law, such as the UNCRC, impact children, youth and families? What tensions do you think would arise as various nations considered the application of Article 8 to this topic?

Among the many social institutions and actors that play an important role in shaping childhood gender and sexuality, the family and its many members often form the first domain of influence. This influence includes individual families and relatives like parents and siblings, but it also includes the broader social and cultural forces that surround each individual family. And within their households and families, children and youth are active agents in their own childhoods as well. The literature and advocacy chronicled throughout this chapter demonstrate the pivotal place of the family in the process of constructing and potentially changing childhood patterns related to gender and sexuality.

Chapter activities

Activity 1: Social forces surrounding parents

The section answering the question 'Who influences parents and families as they think about childhood gender and sexuality' begins by noting that many 'social, cultural, and political forces' influence parents. List the forces you notice from throughout that section, indicating which particular research studies are relevant to each force you listed. Some studies will be relevant to multiple categories.

Activity 2: Social policy and social change

This chapter has highlighted the wide range of forms that change can take. Examples of research detailed throughout the chapter indicate the need for state- and policy-level change. Baptiste and colleagues offer an example of how research can provide the basis for recommendations for change, such as workshop interventions to increase parental involvement in youth HIV prevention. Choose an example of research that underscores unequal parental treatment and, based on the findings of the research you select, outline a recommendation that could be made to policymakers.

Summary

This chapter has:

- Documented the wide range of ways in which parental treatment of sons and daughters contributes to the social construction of children's gender and sexuality, and shapes children's opportunities and experiences;
- Identified a variety of forces that surround parents and in turn shape the way they treat their sons and daughters, including everyday accountability to others, medical and religious authorities, state and public policy and expert advice in parenting books;
- Explored other aspects of families that impact children's gender and sexuality, such as household structure, parental role modelling, exposure to gendered violence and sibling influences;
- Reiterated the importance of children's autonomy and agency, emphasizing the need not to focus only on the one-way influence of parents and other adults on children's gender and sexuality within families.

Further reading

Dugmore, P. and Cocker, C. (2008), 'Legal, social and attitudinal changes: An exploration of lesbian and gay issues in a training programme for social workers in fostering and adoption', *Social Work Education*, 27, 159–68.

Consideration of the changing context of legal rulings in relation to gay and lesbian adoption and foster care placement in the United Kingdom, and report on the effectiveness of a specific training programme for social workers.

Reed, B. W., Cohen-Kettenis, P. T., Reed, T. and Spack, N. (2008), 'Medical care for gender variant young people: Dealing with the practical problems', *Sexologies*, 17, 4, 258–65.

Overview and advice for clinical personnel dealing with gender variant youth and their families in the United Kingdom and elsewhere internationally.

West, C. and Zimmerman, D. (1987), 'Doing gender', *Gender & Society*, 1, 124–51.

Widely cited statement of the theoretical position that gender is an 'interactional accomplishment', constructed socially through interactional processes that include accountability to gendered assessment by other people in everyday settings.

Research details

Differential discipline for sons

Peer-reviewed journal. This study took place in rural Vietnam during two separate periods. In the author Rydstrøm's (2006) words, she 'conducted anthropological fieldwork in order to explore the ways in which children learn to become what is locally considered to be appropriate females or males'. She took field notes on the social interactions of five families, and videotaped conversations for later transcription.

Judgements by others in everyday social interaction

Peer-reviewed journal. In this analysis (Kane, 2006), I conducted interviews with 42 parents (about half mothers and half fathers) of 3- to 5-year-old children. Interviewees came from a variety of race, class and sexual orientation backgrounds, and lived in a variety of family structures (single parents, partnered parents; biological children, foster children, adopted children, stepchildren). Interviews were taped and transcribed.

Public policy shaping sexuality-related parenting practices

Peer-reviewed journal. Baptiste and colleagues (2009) conducted a randomized experiment to test the effects of an intervention on parental involvement in youth HIV prevention in Trinidad and Tobago. 'Parents were recruited mostly via flyers. . . . 180 parent-adolescent dyads (were randomized and) completed workshops and provided data' (498).

The intersection of race, gender and expert advice as parents navigate gender reaffirmation

Peer-reviewed journal. McGuffey (2008) recruited parents for his study at a single therapeutic program for sexually abused boys. Sixty-two parents agreed to participate, with McGuffey taping and transcribing 4–5 interviews with each participant over a multi-year period. The parents were generally of high educational and income status.

The voices of children from lesbian families

Peer-reviewed journal. Conducting eight interviews with children ages 9 to 19 from lesbian-headed households in South Africa, Lubbe (2008) recruited through a snowball sample in which the first participant suggested others. She conducted weekly interviews utilizing 'supportive data creation methods such as collages, time lines, family stories, and artifacts' (330).

Sexual identity rights

Peer-reviewed journal. Chan's (2006) analysis was based on a review of existing research studies about gay, lesbian and bisexual adolescents, as well as detailed analysis of legal cases from multiple nations and international human rights conventions.

Gender, Sexuality and Education

Introduction and key questions

Scholarship and activism related to gender in education traditionally examines equality between boys and girls. But along with the recent trends in gender studies and childhood studies, it has expanded to focus on the diversity of children's experiences, experiences that vary according to gender and sexual identities, as well as intersections of race, class, ability and disability, region and nation, culture and religion. In early years of childhood, families are the primary site for gender refinement and reproduction; upon their entrance to school, children are exposed to new sites of gender reproduction and negotiate a new set of gender norms and expectations. This chapter details levels of gender equality within education, relevant debates on gender issues within education and examples of social change. These topics are discussed with an emphasis on the agency and autonomy of both students and teachers, including attention to activism at international, national and local levels around the world. This chapter is organized around three key questions:

- Do schools treat boys and girls equitably?
- How do schools shape children's gender and sexual identities?
- How do peer cultures within schools refine, reinforce and resist childhood gender and sexuality?

Do schools treat boys and girls equitably?

In many countries, gender equality in education is rooted in the issue of access *to* schools, whereas in countries with widespread access to education at similar levels for boys and girls, gender equality is examined as a matter of what goes on *within* schools. The range in access to education globally is addressed by Birdsall, Levine and Ibrahim (2005), who document that over 100 million primary-school age children are not enrolled in school, 'with the worst shortfalls in Africa and South Asia' (338). In relation to gender equity in access, they go on to note: 'Girls are disproportionately affected, particularly in Sub-Saharan Africa, South Asia, and East Asia and the Pacific' (338). Enrolment variations continue at higher levels of education as well. 'In most developing countries, secondary and other forms of post-primary schooling are heavily slanted towards better-off segments of society- and in most countries towards boys' (Birdsall, Levine and Ibrahim, 2005, 341).

These disparities, both in overall access and in equity of access for girls and boys, are directly connected to poverty and child labour. Bhat (2010) notes that in nations without universal, mandatory and publicly funded education, '[t]he family may depend on the contribution a working child makes to the household income' (325), income a poor family may desperately need. Though education may be associated with future economic opportunity, for poor families in the developing world immediate needs may outweigh such future considerations. As Bhat argues: 'The benefits of going to school are mostly long-term, and will mainly affect the child rather than the parents . . . the costs have to be borne by the parents, and these costs are due in the short-term' (326). But this economic constraint often plays out differently for boys and girls, in that daughters may be expected to earn money to help finance school fees for sons.

NGOs, both large and small, are actively addressing these disparities. Consider, for example, the Education for All (EFA) Movement, initiated by the United Nations Educational, Scientific, and Cultural Organization (UNESCO) in 1990 at the World Conference on Education for All in Jomtien, Thailand. The EFA movement is guided by specific goals for educational access and quality worldwide. The United Republic of Tanzania is one instance of a country where UNESCO's EFA movement has further shaped an effort by the national government to make primary education universal. Following EFA's approach, Tanzania 'is committed to equity and nondiscrimination policies in education and has initiated a series of reforms to ensure equal access to primary education of good quality for all children, to expand secondary education, and to promote education and empowerment of girls' (Okkolin, Lehtomäki and Bhalalusesa, 2010, 64). On the other hand, the specific application of this rights-based approach has generated controversy as well. Some scholars such as Greany (2008) have argued that it does not adequately consider the unique local conditions shaping gendered practices across nations or even across regions within nations, a point she explores through case studies in rural Niger. Though strongly supportive of girls' access to education, Greany advocates for greater attention to local conditions and to competing gender norms in specific contexts. From her perspective, the 'case studies illuminate notions of empowerment or rights through education for women as complex, not following a linear trajectory that could be achieved by a mechanistic granting of a given right' (565).

Key points: UNESCO's EFA goals

UNESCO's website outlines 'internationally agreed education goals' that 'aim to meet learning needs of all children, youth and adults by 2015' (www.unesco.org/en/efa/efa-goals/)

Goal 1: Expanding and improving comprehensive early childhood care and education, especially for the most vulnerable and disadvantaged children.

Goal 2: Ensuring that by 2015 all children, particularly girls, children in difficult circumstances and those belonging to ethnic minorities, have access to, and complete, free and compulsory primary education of good quality.

Goal 3: Ensuring that the learning needs of all young people and adults are met through equitable access to appropriate learning and life-skills programmes.

Goal 4: Achieving a 50 per cent improvement in levels of adult literacy by 2015, especially for women, and equitable access to basic and continuing education for all adults.

⇨

Goal 5: Achieving gender equality in education by 2015, with a focus on ensuring girls' full and equal access to and achievement in basic education of good quality.

Goal 6: Improving all aspects of the quality of education and ensuring excellence of all, so that recognized and measurable learning outcomes are achieved by all, especially in literacy, numeracy and essential life skills.

Key points: Education for young girls in Kenya's largest slum

In Kibera, a slum located outside of Nairobi, Kenya, an estimated 8 per cent of girls have access to an education at some point in their lives. Two young activists, Jessica Posner from the United States and Kennedy Odede from Kenya, co-founded and direct Shining Hope for Communities, an NGO that works to address gender inequality through education. In their own words:

> We combat intergenerational cycles of poverty and gender inequality by linking tuition-free schools for girls to essential social services in Kenya's Kibera slum through a holistic, community-driven approach. By concretely linking essential health and economic services to a school for girls, we demonstrate that benefiting women benefits the whole community, cultivating a community ethos that makes women respected members of society. (www.shininghopeforcommunities.org)

In other countries, especially those in which girls' levels of school access at least equal those of boys, the issue of gender equality in education centres on equal opportunities *within* schools. Research reflects the difficulty in determining who is thriving and who is struggling, as well as when and why these differences exist. In an overview entitled 'Gender inequalities in education', Buchmann, DiPrete and McDaniel (2008) note that it can be difficult to determine the victims of gender achievement gaps and inequalities in education. They document the following trends in the United States:

- Achievement gaps are not objectively clear: studies have found that boys often have higher test scores, while girls often receive higher grades.
- Teachers generally rate girls' classroom behaviours more positively and their effort at schoolwork as greater, a perception that may shape teachers' treatment of and expectations for girls.
- There is a 'female-favourable gap' in post-secondary enrolment, due in part to the changes in the labour market in which gender wage gaps have declined and more women are working in higher-paid positions, which has given women incentive to attend post-secondary schools. Still, men receive higher returns in earnings than women with respect to their education.

- This earnings return differential is likely related to another pattern documented by Gerber and Cheung (2008): Post-secondary course and degree selection patterns continue to be gender segregated, with men more likely than women to pursue higher-paying business and science/math fields.

Gendered patterns have been documented in the United Kingdom as well. For example, Hartley and Sutton (2010) distributed surveys to over 230 children aged 4–10, exploring their perceptions of adult expectations for boys' and girls' classroom performance. The children indicated that they consider girls 'cleverer' and harder working than boys, and they think teachers expect stronger classroom performance from girls. Hartley and Sutton argue that higher teacher expectations reflect gender stereotypes that actually shape outcomes in school, becoming self-fulfilling prophecies that lead girls to more cooperative classroom behaviour and higher grades. In effect, girls may rise to the level of their teachers' expectations while boys may be discouraged by the lower expectations teachers hold of them, prompting them to make less effort and achieve lower results.

While some people believe that biology causes gender differences in educational achievement, arguing for example that boys' minds are wired for science and math and that girls are more capable in English, studies such as Hartley and Sutton's (2010) and many others detailed in this chapter support the social constructionist approach to gender differences highlighted in this book. This approach does not explain gender differences – whether in education or elsewhere in social life – in biological terms, but instead as a result of intersecting social factors. An array of factors – race, ethnicity, class, gender, sexual identities, religion, nationality – can individually mould and intersect to shape one's identity and experiences. Intersecting factors can work together to inhibit or to enable a child's access to and success within school. As scholars, policymakers and activists seek to better understand the inequalities that children face, see to it that children are able to realize their autonomy and agency and ensure that children around the world are granted basic resources, exploring the issue of gender equality in education is critical to progress.

Example of research: Race, class, gender and identity at school

Bettie (2002) conducted ethnographic research in a high school in California, United States, to explore intersections of race/ethnicity, class and gender among white and

Mexican American high school girls. She finds that the white students were more often tracked in advanced courses than Mexican American girls, due to stereotypes of the latter group, which contributed to the upward mobility of white students. But among those who were upwardly mobile, she also found racial/ethnic differences in how they experienced that process of class mobility.

> Whites often do not experience themselves as members of the racial/ethnic category white but as individuals. Without a cultural discourse of class identity, they do not readily experience themselves as members of a class community either. Evidence of this can be seen in the way white, working-class, college prep girls expressed their experience of how education was distancing them from their parents. They did not articulate this as a distancing from their working-class community; their pain was more often articulated in relationship to an individual family, not a people. For white working-class students, this can be an advantage. Their mobility is less complicated because they are not made to feel that they are giving up racial/ethnic or class belonging in the process. (420)

Reflections on the research

Bettie's findings have implications on the institutional level; she explicitly notes their relevance to social and educational policy, namely the importance of bicultural education in addressing the intersecting identities of students – in this case race/ethnicity and class – and in helping students understand 'the possibility of being middle class and maintaining a racial/ethnic identity of color simultaneously' (420).

Activity 1
The girls Bettie (2002) describes are all from working-class families, thus sharing the same starting point of social identity in terms of class and gender. How do their educational experiences shift what they might expect their class identity to become as they grow up, and why – according to Bettie – does that shift feel more complicated to the Mexican American girls than to the white girls?

Activity 2
How does your answer to the previous question document the importance of intersecting identities in shaping upward mobility?

Example of research: Gender and scout camps in four nations

In a comparative study of four nations, Nielsen (2004) explores the consequences of two 'gender models': gender equality (focusing on equal opportunities for males and females) versus gender complementarity (focusing on different opportunities by gender but attempting to value them equally). Nielsen addresses the two models by 'studying children/young people who are in the midst of learning to apply' them (207), relying on observations at scout camps and interviews of scout leaders and

⇨

Example of research – Cont'd

scouts (ages 11–15) in Denmark, Portugal, Slovakia and Russia. Nielsen traces the gender models to socio-political and historical factors in each country, and identifies the role of scout leaders in fostering gender complementarity models in Russian and Portuguese camps versus gender equality models in Slovak and especially Danish camps.

- In Russia, 'the consequence of the complementarity model in this setting is a hierarchical structure created by the visibility of boys' contributions and the invisibility of the girls' (217).
- In Portugal, 'boys are excluded from the female sphere as much as girls are confined to it. At the same time, however, both genders maintain . . . a symbolic hierarchy of gender complementarity that places boys' psychological needs before those of girls' (218–19).
- In Slovak camps, Nielsen argues that boys are dominant, but also that the 'sheer existence of a discourse of gender equality provides girls with a language that they use to formulate their discontent' over their subordination (220).
- In Danish camps, '[t]he girls strive to make themselves allowed to be in the boys' arena' and any 'breach of the equality contract made the Danish girls angry' (222).

Reflections on the research

Nielsen's study highlights the fact that schools are not the only formal settings in which children are educated, with scout camps as just one specific example of an organized setting in which adults convey particular lessons to groups of children.

Activity
Along with scout camps, what other non-school settings do you think educate children about gender expectations?

Key points: Factors associated with gender inequality in education

Research documents that a wide range of factors at various levels shape the extent and contours of gender equality/inequality in education:

- *Socio-political, cultural and historical factors* within a given country or society can shape gender inequality in settings within that society. As previously detailed, Nielsen (2004) reveals how socio-political and historical factors can shape a country's gender model – such as gender equality and gender complementarity – which can then be reproduced in educational settings, such as scout camps.
- *National policy*, such as the US 1972 federal ban on sex discrimination in education known as Title IX, can have a broad impact on the treatment of male and female students. Legal and educational scholars in the United States have demonstrated the continuing impact of the ban – and remaining challenges in its successful implementation – in arenas like equity in school athletic opportunities for girls (Massengale and Lough, 2010), initiatives to encourage girls to pursue science and math education

(Walters and McNeely, 2010) and efforts to reduce sexual harassment in schools (Meyouhas, 2010). Keddle (2009) offers a critical overview of education policy in Australia, beginning with the 1987 National Policy on the Education of Girls, arguing that such policy has not kept pace with changes in feminist politics. In a comparative analysis of how state policy shapes preschool education in Sweden and Scotland, Edstrom (2009) raises questions about the remaining challenges but also reveals the substantial impact of concerted efforts to promote gender equity, whether by emphasizing equity of treatment for girls and boys in Sweden or through policy aimed at addressing underachievement by boys in Scotland.

- *The school-level institutional factors of curriculum and textbooks* can reinforce gender inequalities in schools. A study by Clarke (2005) on twentieth-century Canadian history textbooks documents that portrayals of women in these texts neglect the role, contributions, achievements and suffering of women throughout Canadian history. 'Females are frequently presented off to the side, both actually and metaphorically, of the main story' (256). In a different region of the world, Elgar (2004) analyses the content of science textbooks in Brunei, arguing that her analysis 'reveal(s) a clear gender imbalance in text and illustrations in favour of males' (891).

- *Other school-level institutional factors, like schedules and facilities*, have become the focus of national policy initiatives. In eight nations of the Middle East/North Africa region, Sultana (2008) notes emerging efforts shaped by emphasis on girls rights: 'In Yemen, double shift schooling gives girls the opportunity to do their household chores without having to choose between family demands and education. In Egypt, schools are sensitive to the locale's cultures and needs, and operate on a flexible schedule in response to community economic and seasonal rhythms, allowing girls to accompany their mothers on market days, and during harvest time . . . Other countries/territories (such as Egypt, South Sudan) are making a difference by offering separate bathroom facilities for girls – a simple yet effective way of ensuring parental support to the schooling of their daughters' (132).

- *Family structure*, such as expectations of motherhood, can shape a girl's ability to pursue an education. In an article on the education of girls in Peru, Levison and Moe (1998) explore the impact of family responsibilities, demonstrating that higher levels of such responsibilities are associated with lower school attendance. 'Girls with more preschool age siblings or more adolescent or adult males in the household do more chores and spend less time in school' (352).

- *Interactional factors*, such as teachers' stereotypes or attitudes towards students, can affect how teachers treat students. In a study on children with emotional and behavioural disabilities (EBD) in the United States, Rice and her colleagues (2008) found that counsellors and teachers perceive girls with EBD as more difficult than boys with EBD, an attitude that affects their treatment of the children.

- *Intersectionality* – as documented by Bettie (2002) – can shape students' experiences and achievements in school. Another example comes from Dagkas and Benn's (2006) article 'Young Muslim women's experiences of Islam and physical education in Greece and Britain'. The authors detail British students' greater 'awareness of Islamic requirements for modesty, dress codes and single-sex environments during adolescence' and Greek Muslims' focus on 'a more liberal and integrated, modernist interpretation of being Muslim in the Greek context' (35). Dagkas and Benn argue that the female students' ability to benefit from required physical education curricula was constrained by the intersections of gender, religion, location and cultural contexts.

Schools, education systems and education policy have become sites for debates and evolving discourses related to gender and sexuality worldwide. In some cases, international movements have entered into education debates, and in others, debates within education have permeated a global discourse on children's rights. Even a few examples suggest the range of relevant debates and discourses:

- In 2004, France passed legislation prohibiting students from wearing the hijab, the headscarves often worn by Muslim girls and women, and this ban has sparked controversy. Proponents of the ban argue that it seeks to promote a secular environment in schools and to free Muslim females from the need to wear a headdress, which some interpret as a sexist or oppressive custom. Opponents of the ban argue that it is religious discrimination, stripping girls and women of their religious and gender identities and violating the right to religious expression (Ezekiel, 2006).
- In many countries, the question of whether single-sex schooling is beneficial to students is questioned, researched and debated. Does it improve student learning or problematically segregate boys and girls? Sullivan (2009) explores how single-sex schooling impacts students' academic self-concept in the United Kingdom. 'Boys had higher self-concepts in mathematics and science, and girls in English. Single-sex schooling reduced the gender gap in self-concept' (259). Mbilizi (2008) researches the same question in relation to girls in Malawi, concluding: 'In single-sex schools, girls held higher educational expectations and occupational aspirations for non-traditional careers than in co-educational schools' (223).
- Burns (2008) has documented a new discourse of the 'idealized girl citizen'. According to Burns, educated girls are expected to be 'active agents within an increasingly global world by acquiring a range of entrepreneurial and self-management skills that position them as lifelong learners and as cosmopolitan global consumer-citizens' (355). While this discourse may open new possibilities for girls who have not had full access to formal education, Burns also criticizes its emphasis on global, consumerist, upwardly mobile citizenship rather than local/national autonomy and social justice.

All of these debates indicate the way schools act as important sites crafting gendered opportunities and potentially challenging gender inequalities, but in ways that cannot be easily measured nor separated from the intersections of gender with other dimensions of inequality. There are no simple answers to whether banning headscarves in schools frees Muslim girls or discriminates against them, whether globalized citizenship offers girls new access to international opportunities or cuts them off from their local or national communities or whether single-sex schooling offers boys and girls the chance to excel academically or reinforces gendered divisions. But as societies debate these questions, the resulting arguments highlight the critical role that educational institutions and educational policies play in childhood gender, and the difficulties involved in defining what constitutes equitable educational treatment for boys and girls from varying backgrounds.

How do schools shape children's gender and sexual identities?

Many of the studies noted so far suggest the various ways in which schools shape the gender and sexual identities of students. Table 5.1 offers an overview of additional research findings, with specific attention to the potential impact of teacher behaviour, curriculum and school climate.

Table 5.1 Selected research findings on the impacts of school curricula and structures on students' gender and sexual identities and experiences

Author(s)	Location of research, age range of children and research method	Observed classroom activities and curriculum	Conclusions and implications
Martin (1998)	USA 3- to 5-year-old students Semi-structured field observations in five preschool classrooms	Observed a 'hidden curriculum' in preschools that teaches students how to behave as little boys and little girls (boys allowed greater physical range, girls subtly directed to be calm)	The process of disciplining bodies in preschools is intertwined with gendering bodies; 'gendered physicalities are not natural, nor are they easily and straightforwardly acquired' (510)
Røthing (2008)	Norway 15- and 16-year-old students Observations of tenth grade classrooms in three public schools	Norway's national curriculum on homosexuality is designed to foster what the author calls 'homotolerance' (acceptance of a variety of sexual orientations, including non-heterosexual orientations)	Concludes that 'even though education on homosexuality may create increased homotolerance, the very same education does also marginalize and stigmatize homosexuality as well as reproduce binary and heteronormative concepts of sexuality' (253)

Table 5.1 Continued

Author(s)	Location of research, age range of children and research method	Observed classroom activities and curriculum	Conclusions and implications
Meyer (2008)	Canada Teachers In-depth interviews with six Canadian teachers about their responses to gender harassment and bullying among students	Highlighted how teachers' responses 'vary on the basis of teachers' identities and experiences in their school cultures, but in all cases in this study, the barriers outweigh the motivators for intervention' (567)	Emphasizes the need for school leaders to make structural changes; without these changes teachers may not have the proper tools or resources to intervene
Dukmak (2010)	United Arab Emirates Boys and girls, 10–12 years old in three groups – high achieving students, low achieving students and students with learning disabilities Observations in fourth grade and special education classrooms	Explored classroom interactions; among all achievement/disability levels, boys initiated more interactions with teachers than girls did and teachers initiated more student interactions with boys than with girls	Boys may receive more opportunities for academic success due to their greater confidence in initiating interaction with teachers and their greater likelihood of receiving teachers' attention.
Teixeira, Villani and do Nascimento (2008)	Brazil Male and female students ages 15–17 Observations at classroom events	Observed the different behaviour of male and female students in the classroom: boys' focus on their masculine identities and girls' need for approval, attention and affirmation	'In Brazil we need to re-think a classroom structure, which currently leads to a permissive environment for boys where they can exercise their 'macho' power not only over girls but also over teachers' (396)

Example of research: Gender, sexuality and HIV/AIDS education

In a 2009 study in South Africa, Bhana explores the role of gender and sexuality in HIV education in two Durban primary schools. Bhana analyses 'life-skills' lessons, focusing on the pedagogies and discourses that shape what students learn. Her evidence contains excerpts from classroom conversations between students and teachers during life-skills lessons. The teachers focus on transmission – rarely, if ever, referring to sexual transmission – and the care of HIV-infected persons, and neglect to incorporate issues of gender, sex and sexuality into the classroom discussion.

> The pedagogical approaches at both schools did not engage with the cultures, lives and identities of young children, short-circuiting children's opportunities to develop into critical thinkers. Important in HIV/AIDS education is the forum for children to openly discuss HIV/AIDS, sexuality and gender . . . The social ramification of HIV/AIDS is evident in the ways teachers address issues around stigma, discrimination and discourses of care, and the ways in which discourses of sexuality are ignored, overlooked and silenced. (176)

Bhana suggests that teacher-training programmes could affect a valuable pedagogical shift in structuring HIV/AIDS education curriculum and programmes to highlight the relevance of social stigma and other social issues to HIV/AIDS.

Reflections on the research

Activity

Bhana concludes that 'pedagogical practice should tap into the rich potential of children, acknowledging their agency and sparking off discussion that can address divisive gender and other social inequalities reinforced by the epidemic' (176). How might schools like the ones in Bhana's study approach this? What kind of impact might any approaches you come up with have on the perspectives of a new generation of South Africans?

Interview with Deevia Bhana about her research on HIV/AIDS education in South Africa

Deevia Bhana is Associate Professor in the School of Education at the University of KwaZulu-Natal in South Africa. Her current research continues to focus on gender, childhood sexualities and AIDS.

Emily Kane:	What surprised you the most about the process of conducting your research on HIV/AIDS education in Durban schools, or about the results?
Deevia Bhana:	Overall, I was not surprised. In previous work conducted with teachers in the early years many had said that gender and sexuality were not relevant to young children. However, I was surprised that the teachers were able to regulate sexuality education in the ways that they did. The teacher in the township school kept saying s-word instead of sex when talking to me. The teacher in the former white school deliberately cut out the picture that made reference to AIDS and sex, as she thought it was not appropriate for the children.
Emily Kane:	You have continued to explore other aspects of gender and sexuality in educational settings since this article on HIV/AIDS education. Could

you briefly describe your more recent work and how you see it as connecting to or differing from the article featured as an example here?

Deevia Bhana: I have maintained my focus on younger children but I am also focusing on older teenagers with specific emphasis on gender, sexuality and childhood studies against the backdrop of AIDS. Extending the regulation of sexuality and restricting comprehensive sexuality education, I have found that South African teachers construct teenage pregnancy with shame and ostracize pregnant mothers, against the constitution of the country, and in doing so teachers try to wish innocence on schooling contexts and remove any evidence of contamination. However, teachers do not monolithically subscribe to this view and there is evidence of changing patterns of conduct. Also, further evidence from young children in the early years of schooling illustrates their widespread knowledge of sex and AIDS but young children are careful not to articulate this knowledge to adult teachers as they have sophisticated understandings of sex as taboo and the age specific norm in relation to such knowledge.

Scholars have also highlighted the impact of extra-curricular activities and programs – such as after school programs, interventions and sports – on shaping children's gender and sexual identities. Studies document positive impacts of extra-curricular programs and interventions on the development of children's gender and sexual identities.

- In a study on peer-directed, active-learning interventions in the United States, Lamb and colleagues (2009) suggest that youth who participated in an intervention were far more likely than those who did not participate to confront sexist remarks, although these youth did not change their 'personal gender role beliefs' (378).
- In a research project exploring singing in Australian schools, and how hegemonic masculinity discourages boys' interest in singing, Hall (2005) found that 'the genesis of the "missing male" trend in singing at school may be occurring in early childhood', suggesting 'the importance of finding strategies to support boys' success in singing long before adolescence' (5).
- In an overview of new research, Horn and colleagues (2009) note that as LGBT youth in the United States face particular development processes, there is potential for programmes to provide support during sexual identity development of these youth, who often 'remain invisible in "mainstream" youth programs' (864).
- In Jordan, music performances of high school students have provided adolescent girls with the opportunity to explore 'patriotism, the proper way to live their faith, and their role as young women in contemporary Jordan' (Adely, 2007, 1663). Adely concludes that extra-curricular activities like music allow adolescent girls to engage creatively with a range of questions about their identities and role in society.

Both in and outside of the classroom, schools play a significant role in shaping a child's gender and sexual identity. While in many cases scholars highlight the hidden biases of curriculum, classroom rules and teachers, it is also important to consider that schools have the ability to foster tolerance and support for students.

School climates – shaped by institutional-level structures, administrators and teachers and peer cultures – offer another way in which students' gender and sexualities are shaped in schools. Later in this chapter, the role of peer cultures within schools will be explored in more detail. However, it is relevant to briefly outline the role of school climates in students' experiences in this section. Positive school climates have been tied to lower levels of homophobic teasing, and for gay, lesbian and questioning students, lower levels of thoughts of depression, suicidality, alcohol and marijuana use and truancy (Birkett, Espelage and Koenig, 2009, 997). Teacher attitudes towards and treatment of students encourage gender stereotypical behaviours and shape the development of students' gender and sexual identities, as suggested in Martin's (1998) exploration of the 'hidden curriculum' in preschools (see Table 5.1). In cases of gender harassment and bullying where intervention may be appropriate, teachers can also struggle with a lack of agency due to institutional barriers, as documented in Meyer (2008). This lack of agency among teachers is impacted by, and impacts, a school's climate, which in turn affects students' gender and sexual identities, particularly among students who experience gender harassment and bullying.

Student activism in schools can provide an avenue for 'a proactive response to a context that may be characterized by hostility, but through which empowerment can be achieved' (Horn and colleagues, 2009, 864). For example, sexual orientation-related activism provides an opportunity to spread awareness of issues and inequalities that LGBT students face. LGBT activism has taken the form of student groups, campaigns, policy and legislation. Student groups, such as gay–straight alliances, have become increasingly common across the United States since the first GSA was established in 1972 (Johnson, 2007). In addition to GSAs, other campaigns and networks spread awareness of inequalities and gay student issues, such as the Gay, Lesbian, and Straight Education Network (GLSEN), a US education organization that works with students, teachers, parents and others to address gender and sexual orientation inequalities and discrimination in schools (www.glsen.org).

How do peer cultures within schools refine, reinforce and resist childhood gender and sexuality?

As students grow older, peer cultures within schools play an increasing role, reflecting children's agency and autonomy – students begin to have a larger impact on the development of one another as peer cultures take on a life of their own. Literature on peer cultures within schools focuses on the relationship between gender and sexuality, and on the notion that in most cases, peer cultures are characterized by heteronormativity, or the taken-for-granted assumption that everyone is and should be heterosexually identified. Though Chapter 7 addresses children's peer cultures more broadly, this section highlights some brief examples relevant to schools in particular. Researchers have documented a host of institutional, interactional and intersecting factors that shape a school's peer cultures, which in turn shape students' experiences of gender and sexuality.

- Anthropologist Brison (2009) notes that rural children in Fiji play in mixed-gender groups of familiar peers, but kindergarten attendance leads to segregation by gender as the children attempt to navigate a larger, unfamiliar peer group. This segregation then leads to more distinct gendered peer cultures for the children.
- Ferfolja (2007) highlights the institutional processes in Australia that help allow peer cultures to marginalize non-heterosexual students: such as the absence of gay and lesbian issues in school policies; the restriction of textbooks that address gay and lesbian issues; and the failure to address abusive anti-lesbian/gay language.
- Portelli (2006) addresses the way school curriculum and teacher behaviour in Malta intersect with peer cultures to enforce a particular kind of masculinity among boys. He argues that masculinity is expressed for many through a preference for speaking Maltese and a practice of peer teasing of boys who speak English, especially if they also fail to participate in sports and popular music subcultures locally dominant among male students.
- Baker-Sperry (2007) observes US school reading groups discussing Walt Disney's *Cinderella*. 'The girls embraced the story, identified with the female characters, and actively engaged in filtering the text through their lived experience and expectations for the future' (725) resulting in peer pressure that reinforces expectations and stereotypes of femininity within the classroom.
- Jackson and Dempster (2009) illustrate how peer cultures and hegemonic masculinity in the United Kingdom result in the 'effortless achievement' and 'uncool to work' discourses of male students, discourses that exist in high schools as

well as in higher education: 'Young male undergraduates emphasised that to be "accepted" they needed to socialise and not be overly conscientious in their approach to study' (351).

As these various examples highlight, peer cultures shape children's gender and sexuality, often reinforcing gender separation, traditional gendered behaviour and heteronormative pressures. But those peer cultures are also allowed, encouraged or shaped by other institutional and interactional forces such as media, curriculum and teacher expectations.

Example of research: Masculinity in the kindergarten classroom

Jordan and Cowan (1995) explore 'what happens when children encounter the expectations of the school within their already established conceptions of gender' (728). The study is based on observation in an Australian kindergarten classroom and focuses on the warrior narratives in which boys engage: '[N]arratives that assume that violence is legitimate and justified when it occurs within a struggle between good and evil'. While in the classroom free play was encouraged, the teacher discouraged warrior narratives, leading to 'a contest between two definitions of masculinity: what we have chosen to call "warrior narratives" and the discourses of civil society – rationality, responsibility, and decorum – that are the basis of school discipline' (728). The pre-existing peer culture of boys and girls was both impacted by, and impacted, teacher treatment of students – the teacher intervened in cases where boys engaged with warrior narratives, but did not intervene when girls quietly played in the doll corner. Thus the girls experienced their peer culture as validated by the school, while boys experienced the school setting as discouraging their preferred enactments of gender.

Reflections on the research

Activity

In Jordan and Cowan's study, the teacher intervened to discipline boys in the context of their warrior narratives, but did not intervene with girls' playtime in the doll corner. How might these teacher interventions, or lack of intervention, disadvantage both boys and girls?

Example of research: Openly gay school athletes

Anderson (2002) investigated the experiences of openly gay athletes on school sports teams in the United States. Anderson's study is based on qualitative interviews with gay student athletes, over half of whom were open about their sexual orientation. In his words: 'I look to sport as a site of contestation for the construction and reproduction
⇨

Example of research – Cont'd

of masculinity by qualitatively investigating how gay athletes challenge orthodox assumptions of masculinity by publicly coming out as gay within their high school or collegiate athletic teams' (861). Anderson focuses on primarily heterosexual sports teams, and demonstrates that many openly gay male athletes have positive experiences on their teams, especially if they are strong players. Still, they felt pressure to conform to a heteronormative framework: '[T]he informants in this study were victimized by heterosexual hegemony and largely maintained a heteronormative framework by self-silencing their speech and frequently engaged in heterosexual dialogue with their teammates' (874). In Anderson's study, athletes' expressions of sexuality are shaped by the peer culture of their teammates, with heterosexual athletes able to express their sexuality while their openly gay peers are expected not to do so.

Reflections on the research

Anderson comments on how the acceptance of openly gay athletes as team members illustrates teams as a site of tolerance – even though gay teammates on dominantly heterosexual teams may not be accepted *as* gay, they are accepted as athletes.

Activity

Based on your own experiences or the experiences of others you know, what role do you think sports, and other extra-curricular activities, can play in changing the gender and sexuality-related peer culture within schools?

Both of these examples of research, from the kindergarten classroom in Australia to the high school and college level in the United States, highlight the way pressures shaping gender and sexuality for children and youth within schools span across age and geography, and play out in both the classroom and extra-curricular realms. Along with the many studies discussed throughout this chapter, these examples also indicate that a variety of actors, such as teachers, coaches, administrators and peers and a variety of structures, such as curriculum, classroom facilities, funding and policies, are important to consider in understanding how gender and sexuality are shaped in educational settings.

Chapter activities

Activity 1: Examining intersectionality in schooling experiences

Throughout this chapter, examples of research, such as Bettie (2002) and Dagkas and Benn (2006), illustrate how intersectionality can shape students' experiences in schools. Look back through the other studies highlighted in examples of research, charts and lists throughout this chapter. How does intersectionality impact children in these other studies?

⇨

Activity 2: Acting on inequality

Throughout this chapter, schools are addressed not only as sites of gender refinement, reinforcement and reproduction, but also as sites for action and activism in the face of unequal educational experiences. Consider the research presented throughout the chapter. Select a piece of research you found interesting and think of ways in which one might act on the inequalities revealed. Briefly outline a campaign, student group or some form of action that might be able to address the gender inequalities in education revealed in the study you selected.

Summary

This chapter has:

- Discussed the complexity of defining gender inequality in education, and how perspectives on its extent and origins vary;
- Examined key issues, debates and trends related to gender and sexuality in education;
- Explored the role of teachers, curriculum, textbooks, national- and school-level policies and peer cultures within schools in shaping, reinforcing, refining and resisting gender and sexual identities;
- Highlighted examples of gender and sexuality-related activism in education at the grassroots, national and international levels.

Further reading

Bayne, E. (2009), 'Gender pedagogy in Swedish preschools', *Gender Issues*, 26, 2, 130–40.
History of gender equity initiatives in Swedish preschools: Their origins, how they have changed over time, their successes and limitations, as well as suggestions for future consideration.

Kumashiro, K., Baber, S. A., Richardson, E., Ricker-Wilson, C. and Wong, P. L. (2004), 'Preparing teachers for anti-oppressive education: International movements', *Teaching Education*, 15, 3, 257–75.
Overview of teacher education initiatives in Asia, Africa, North America and South America, including attention to gender and sexuality-related efforts, and the political obstacles faced by such initiatives.

Pascoe, C. J. (2007), *Dude, you're a fag: Masculinity and sexuality in high school*. Berkeley, CA: University of California Press.
A widely cited observational study of the intersections of gender and sexuality in a US high school, focusing on how high school boys interactionally enforce gender expectations by using discourses about sexuality.

Research details

Race, class, gender and identity at school

Peer-reviewed journal. Bettie (2002) conducted ethnographic research in a high school in an agricultural area of California. The school had about 60 per cent white and 40 per cent Mexican American students. Bettie used both observations and formal interviews to illustrate the intersections among race, class and gender, and how these intersections can enable and inhibit girls' achievements in schools.

Gender and scout camps in four nations

Peer-reviewed journal. Nielsen's (2004) analysis is based on observations at scout camps and interviews of leaders and scouts in Denmark, Portugal, Slovakia and Russia. Contact with the selected camps was facilitated through an organization called the World Organization of the Scout Movement, and all of these nations have gender-integrated scouting groups.

Gender, sexuality and HIV/AIDS education

Peer-reviewed journal. Bhana (2009) bases her analysis of HIV education on detailed observations of 'life-skills' lessons at two South African primary schools, both in Durban but with differing student populations. The observation focused on the pedagogies and discourses that shape what students learn.

Masculinity in the kindergarten classroom

Peer-reviewed journal. Jordan and Cowan's (1995) research consists of open-ended, non-participant observation during weekly visits to a kindergarten classroom in a suburban area of Australia. The selected school enrolled students from a wide range of socio-economic backgrounds; the classroom was led by a teacher regarded as non-traditional in her approach to gender.

Openly gay school athletes

Peer-reviewed journal. Anderson (2002) conducted qualitative interviews with 42 gay athletes on high school and college teams, and focused in this article on the 26 who were open with their teammates about their sexual orientation. The interviewees came from a wide range of sports, and from various regions of the United States (they were recruited through e-mail list servers).

Gender, Sexuality and Media

6

Chapter Outline

Introduction and key questions

Media and consumption are sites that draw significant attention from activists and scholars focused on childhood gender and sexuality. This includes attention to the content and impact of messages imbedded in various media texts, as well as children's agency in responding to those messages. Though media form the primary topic of this chapter, advertising and the consumption that advertisers seek to shape are closely linked to media, and thus are considered as well. Organized around three key questions, the chapter addresses a range of scholarship on the impact of the media on children and highlights examples of activism among organizations dedicated to media accountability and education through media texts:

- What kinds of messages about gender and sexuality are found in children's media?
- What impact do media messages have on children?
- How do children interpret, refine and resist media messages?

What kinds of messages about gender and sexuality are found in children's media?

This fundamental question makes a good starting point for exploring gender and sexuality in children's media. Around the world and across types of media – movies, television, books, magazines, video games, music – researchers have documented many aspects of media content related to gender and sexuality. While the specific patterns vary and have changed somewhat over time, the general tendency remains: much media content over-represents males, particularly white males, and features them in roles that are more active and positive, while females are more likely to be represented as passive and in traditional care-taking, appearance-oriented or sexualized roles. As Baker-Sperry and Grauerholz (2003) conclude in their analysis of the classic German fairy tales of the Brothers Grimm, after assessing which of these tales have persisted in popular form today, 'findings suggest that feminine beauty is a dominant theme and that tales with heavy emphases on feminine beauty are much more likely to have survived' (711). From colouring books in the United States (Fitzpatrick and McPherson, 2010) to the commercials shown on children's television in Poland and the United Kingdom (Furnham and Saar, 2005), scholars have found that male characters dominate, and are more often depicted as active agents. Media content also tends to reinforce heteronormativity. Table 6.1 offers an overview of some of the many studies documenting these patterns.

Table 6.1 Selected research findings on images of gender and sexuality in children's media

Author(s)	Location of research Media type	Research method and research focus	Patterns documented and implications/conclusions
Al-Shehab (2008)	Kuwait Children's television programming	Content analysis focused on gender and racial/ethnic representations on Kuwaiti national television and an Egyptian satellite channel	Programming reinforced gender and race stereotypes by under-representing female characters and non-white, non-Arab and Asian characters; most characters 'acted within narrowly defined gender roles' (60), which the author argues 'may inculcate mistaken gender role understanding in children' (61)

Table 6.1 Continued

Author(s)	Location of research Media type	Research method and research focus	Patterns documented and implications/conclusions
Neto and Furnham (2005)	Portugal Children's television advertisements	Content analysis of television commercials with attention to gender and ethnicity	Male characters outnumbered females and were more likely to be shown in active roles, but authors also conclude that gender stereotyping is less evident in advertising on children's television than adult television in Portugal and may be declining further over time
Martin and Kazyak (2009)	Internationally distributed mainstream G-rated children's films	Content analysis of films with focus on their depiction of heterosexuality	Heterosexuality assumed and celebrated; 'heterosexuality is constructed through hetero-romantic love relationships as exceptional, powerful, magical, and transformative' and 'men gazing desirously at women's bodies' (315)
Williams, Martins, Consalvo and Ivory (2009)	USA Video games	Content analysis of characters in video games, analysing their gender, race and age	Video game representation follows similar patterns to those documented for television: 'systematic over-representation of males, whites, and adults' (815)
Hamilton, Anderson, Broaddus and Young (2006)	USA Children's picture books	Content analysis of 200 popular picture books; included both prize-winning books and more general titles; focus on gender patterns in characters' occupations and characteristics	Across all book types, children's books continue to reinforce gender stereotypes by under-representing female characters and showing them in domestic and nurturing roles or traditionally female occupations
Sengupta (2006)	Canada Magazines for adolescent girls	Content analysis of advertisements, with attention to gender, race and product advertised	Results reflect the prevalence of stereotypes: 'white beauty ideal, hypersexual Black women', 'technologically savvy East Asians' (799)

Interview with Karin Martin about her research on sexuality and childhood in the United States

Karin Martin is Professor of Sociology at the University of Michigan – Ann Arbor, United States. She teaches courses on gender, sexuality, childhood and qualitative methods.

Emily Kane: What surprised you the most about the process of conducting your research on heterosexiness in G-rated films, or about the results?

Karin Martin: What surprised me most was finding heteronormativity working through the exalting of heterosexuality. As a gender and sexuality scholar I was familiar with the theoretical accounts that described heteronormativity as including the taken for granted nature of heterosexuality, the ways in which heterosexuality is mundane, normal, uncommented upon, and so on. Yet, this is in many ways the opposite of what many G-rated films portray to the children who watch them. Heterosexual relationships in these films are not mundane and everyday. They are exciting, adventurous, magical and transformative. The question remains whether making heterosexuality magical and transformative is something particular to children's culture or if it is something we learn from children's culture and can use to further elaborate our understanding of heteronormativity more generally. My hunch is that it is the latter and that this finding adds to our understanding of heteronormativity and suggests that context matters in how heterosexuality becomes normalized and for whom.

Emily Kane: Your work with various colleagues has been cited throughout this book, including articles focused on the influence of parents, teachers, experts and media. At the same time, you also recognize children's agency and autonomy throughout your work. Could you comment briefly on how you think about the balance between adult-generated influences on children and their own agency as you craft new research projects?

Karin Martin: In my research I have struggled with how to balance, understand and study children as social actors. I take very seriously the 'new' sociology of childhood's critique of the view of socialization that treats children as empty vessels to be filled by parents, schools and media. In my research I want both to recognize the power parents and other social actors have in children's lives while attending to how children themselves are actors. I think my struggle with this has stemmed from the fact that I study very young children – preschoolers – and that I am interested in how they learn about sexuality. Parents, teachers, human subject boards and funders are all (understandably in many ways) wary of a researcher who wants to interview their preschoolers about sexuality or observe a hidden curriculum of sexuality in their classroom or the like. This has made it very difficult for me to get the voices and understandings of children into my work. I think, however, that I have recently found a way around this. I am currently completing a project in which I gave 50 parents from two local preschools a bag with an audio recorder, a short survey and four books about 'where babies come from' and asked them to read and talk about one of the books (which ranged from simple to comprehensive to Christian-oriented) with their child at home. The parents audio-recorded these conversations; the conversations have been transcribed; and I am now working on an analysis of these data. The preliminary analyses have captured what I hoped they would: both that parents have tremendous power to foreclose conversations about sexuality *and* that children elicit information and shape these conversations about sexuality.

Music popular with adolescents has also been the subject of analysis by researchers interested in the gendered messages in media, as the two examples below document in very different geographical locations.

Examples of research: Gender, sexuality and music

Songs, chants and children's sexual agency

Izugbara (2005) uses field observation and focus groups to explore the role of musical verses in shaping local understandings of gender and sexuality in a Nigerian study addressing not mass media but local traditions. Recognizing boys as active agents in shaping their own peer culture, Izugbara seeks to illuminate 'the role of the verses in defining the erotic spaces and meanings on the basis of which young boys organize, constitute, and base their sexual conducts' (55). After identifying a series of songs and chants that were well known among the boys, Izugbara goes on to explore their impact. Though respectful of the songs and chants as elements of the boys' peer cultures and a potential source of positive sexual education and agency, Izugbara concludes that the verses express and construct a 'heady mixture of paternalism, aggression, systematic subordination of women . . . coupled with a rejection of homosexuality' and 'condemn female autonomy and agency' (72).

Objectification of women in popular song lyrics

Music conveyed through mass media in the United States is the subject of a research study completed by Bretthauer, Zimmerman and Banning (2006). They studied the lyrics of 100 popular, commercially distributed songs, identifying six separate gender-related themes that emerged across the lyrics. They argue that common among these themes is an emphasis on men's power over women, the treatment of women as objects and violence against women. With an audience primarily made up of adolescents, Bretthauer and colleagues consider the lyrics of these songs to send powerful messages about gender and heterosexual relationships.

Examples of research – Cont'd

Reflections on the research

These studies draw similar conclusions despite their very different geographic locations and their emphasis on local versus mass-marketed music. Treating songs as texts that convey social meanings, the authors of both articles argue that music enjoyed by adolescents can reinforce heterosexuality as well as traditional gender inequalities, celebrating male power, strength and control while casting girls and women in passive, subordinate roles.

Activity

Pick a popular song that you remember from your youth, and search the internet for the lyrics (there are a variety of song lyrics sites on the internet, such as www.azlyrics. com). Print out the lyrics, jot notes in the margins about any gender or sexuality related messages you think the lyrics convey and then reflect on what impact – if any – you think these lyrics may have had on your ideas about gender and sexuality.

Like analyses of music as a cultural text, studies about adolescent sexuality and sexual health in the media generally find at least some gender differentiation as well.

- Joshi, Peter and Valkenburg (2011) investigate the messages about sexuality in Dutch magazines for teenage girls, and compare them to messages in similar magazines in the United States. Analysing over 600 articles with sex-related content, they drew a more positive conclusion about female sexuality, finding a relatively equitable balance of attention to boys' and girls' sexual pleasure in the magazines sampled in both nations. In terms of what they call 'sexual wanting' on the other hand, boys were depicted as more interested in sex than girls in the US magazines, while in the Dutch magazines a similar level of sexual wanting was represented for both boys and girls.
- Hust, Brown and L'Engle (2008) analysed the sex-related content in US television shows, magazines, movies and music identified by a large sample of 12–14 year olds, and discovered that 'less than one half of 1% of the content included information about or depictions of sexually healthy behaviour' (4). They go on to look in detail at the small handful of such depictions, and express concern that many are inaccurate or 'reinforced traditional gender stereotypes that males seek sex and females are responsible for protection against pregnancy' (4).
- Bryant (2010) acknowledges youth sexual agency and the need to respect adolescents' desire for sexual information, but critically analyses the potential effects of exposure to violent pornographic media on Australian youth. Her review of a wide range of research studies indicates that boys are much more likely than girls to be exposed to such media, particularly through the internet, and she argues that in some cases it has the potential to encourage objectification of girls and women.

Not all content analyses of media texts for children highlight traditional or stereotypical media messages. Along with the change over time some of the studies discussed so far document, other scholars have focused specifically on how media content resists traditional gender stereotypes, sometimes in terms of implicit messages. Dennis (2009) offers an example in his article 'The boy who would be queen: Hints and closets on children's television'. He concedes that US television programming for children and teens rarely offers open acknowledgement of non-heterosexual characters. But his study of three widely available children's cable television networks also 'revealed many examples of resistance to the heteronormative ideology: intimate same-sex friendships; inclusive statements . . .; scenes that hint at the existence of same-sex desire; gender-transgressive or otherwise gay-stereotyped characters; and jokes and references that require a knowledge of gay culture' (738).

Example of research: Star Wars and masculinities

Bettis and Sternod (2009) offer a close reading of the messages about masculinity in the six films of the hugely successful Star Wars series, focusing on social change over the 15 years between the first set of three films (released between 1977 and 1983) and the second set (released between 1998 and 2005). With attention to the inter-sections of race and class with gendered representations, they argue that the central character of the second trilogy, Anakin Skywalker, can be read as rejecting hegemonic masculinity. '. . . the contradictions between the man Anakin is becoming (emotional and loving) and the man the Jedi want him to be (controlled and stoic) cause him to rethink the hegemonic norms in which he was trained' (33). Bettis and Sternod go on to contend that Anakin's violent disfiguration in the final instalment demonstrates that 'men and boys who reject the dominant mode of masculinity put themselves at risk' (34). Though they consider other readings as well, a reminder that media content is open to multiple interpretations (a topic considered more fully in the third key question of this chapter), their argument that the films offer a critique of hegemonic masculinity is an interesting one to contemplate.

Reflections on the research

Most of the more traditional social science research reviewed in this chapter uses content analysis to measure the frequency of gender stereotypes and gender imbalances in representation in media texts. Bettis and Sternod's approach is not one of counting, but rather reading the same text in several different ways. As they put it, 'popular films can be read in multiple ways because they contain multiple and contradictory meanings' (22).

Activity

Select a popular film with a target audience that includes children or adolescents, and that you think has some kind of gender or sexuality related meanings. Briefly outline at least two different readings one might offer in terms of messages the film sends about gender or sexuality.

What impact do media messages have on children?

Many of the studies reviewed so far discuss potential *impacts* of media messages, even if they are focused more on detailing the *content*. Media content is significant to the degree we assume it has some impact, of course, and so all of these authors comment on the effect media messages may have in shaping children's understanding of gender and sexuality. Even a few examples paint a clear picture of the potential impact:

- Al-Shehab (2008) on Kuwaiti television for children: '. . . children may think that in real life all males and whites are heroes, leaders, independent, rescuers, active and responsible, while females, nonwhites, and non-Arabs are dependent, submissive, followers, romantic, passive and so on' (60).
- Martin and Kazyak (2009) on US G-rated films for children: 'Both ordinary and exceptional constructions of heterosexuality work to normalize its status because it becomes difficult to imagine anything other than this form of social relationship or anyone outside its bonds' (333).
- Sengupta (2006) on magazines for adolescent girls in Canada: '. . . negative stereotypes (in magazine images) can have an impact on social reality by reinforcing or building on expectations of certain social groups. These reinforced stereotypes may, in turn, contribute to prejudice and unequal educational and occupational opportunities' (807).

Along with these discussions about implications based on studies focused primarily on content, some scholars explicitly address the impact of gender and sexuality-related messages in their approach to data collection. For example, Selfhout, Delsing, ter Bogt and Meeus (2008) use survey data from over 900 Dutch adolescents gathered at two points in time to document that listening to heavy metal and hip-hip music is associated with subsequent increases in violent and anti-social behaviour among boys (but less so for girls). Kaestle, Halpern and Brown (2007) reach a similar conclusion with an even more specific outcome measured. Their survey data from about 900 US children in the age group 12–15 shows that 'exposure to televised music videos and pro wrestling were associated with rape acceptance (lower levels of agreeing with the statement 'forcing a partner to have sex is never OK') among males, but not females' (185). Interviews with children are included in Lewin-Jones and Mitra's (2009) research on British television commercials for children.

Combining a content analysis of advertisements that documented greater presence and activity of male characters with the voices of children through interviews, they conclude that a 'link can be established between the polarity that exists within commercials and children's own perceptions of gender roles and behavior' (47).

Gender-linked body image issues have received scholarly attention in terms of media impact as well. Esnaola, Rodriguez and Goni (2010) draw on survey data from Spain to document that exposure to social modeling from media is negatively associated with body satisfaction for both male and female adolescents, but especially so for females. They argue that this association has implications for negative outcomes such as low self-esteem and eating disorders. Though more research has focused on girls, particularly in relation to eating disorders like anorexia and bulimia, steroid abuse among teenage boys and young men has received increasing focus too. As Esnaola and colleagues put it, 'the male beauty ideal of a lean yet muscular body is becoming an important issue for men, with poor body image sometimes leading to the adoption of numerous health-threatening behaviors, such as the use of steroids, ephedrine and deleterious dieting strategies' (21). Baird and Grieve (2006), in a study of US college-age adolescent men, link these tendencies to media exposure. They found that viewing advertisements with male models, rather than only products, was associated with decreased body satisfaction for young men.

Example of research: Race, gender and media messages about beauty

Gordon (2008) set out to measure the impact of media on African American girls, focusing on their attitudes towards the importance of appearance and beauty. Based on survey data from girls ages 13–17, Gordon explores exposure to what she calls 'Black-oriented' television programmes, songs/song lyrics and music videos as media genres and the girls' appearance-related attitudes. She is particularly interested in how important 'being (physically) attractive' is to the girls themselves and how important they think it is to girls' futures more generally. Most of Gordon's conclusions are consistent with previous research, documenting that 'exposure to and identification with media portrayals of Black women as sex objects whose value is based on their appearance may contribute to African American girls' emphasizing beauty and appearance, either in their own lives or for girls in general' (253). She concludes her article by hoping her findings 'will spark continued exploration of how media portrayals can limit African American girls' conceptions of who they are and what should be important in their lives' (255).

⇨

> ### Example of research – Cont'd
> ### Reflections on the research
> #### Activity
> Gordon suggests that media portrayals of African American girls and women have implications for youth media consumers. While we may not always be able to change what is portrayed in the media, we have the agency to influence how these portrayals are interpreted and to think critically about how these portrayals impact our lives. Jot a few notes about some ways one might be able to spread awareness and start conversations that remind media consumers of their agency to determine how media messages influence their lives.

Closely related to the gendering messages in mass media is the world of marketing and consumption, a particularly clear link in that much commercial media is funded by advertising. In this arena too, scholars have identified gender and sexuality-related impacts on youth. Cook and Kaiser (2004) use interviews and historical analysis to demonstrate the way marketers constructed a particular phase of childhood for girls, the 'tween' years, as part of an effort to define a market segment in the fashion industry. Calling this 'tween' period 'an ambiguous, age-delineated marketing and merchandising category' (203), they go on to note:

> This category tends to produce and reproduce a 'female consuming subject' who has generally been presumed to be white, middle or upper middle class and heterosexual. Building upon historical materials, we focus much of our efforts on analyzing contemporary cultural commercial iterations of the tween as they have arisen since the early 1990s, a time when clothing makers and entrepreneurs of childhood redoubled their efforts to define a market semantic space for the tween on the continuum of age-based goods and meanings. (203)

Russell and Tyler (2005) build on Cook and Kaiser's work in a study that includes interviews with adolescent girls in the United Kingdom. These authors explore girls' agency and the role of media and marketing in shaping their gendered identities through consumption. In an innovative research design, they sent a group of girls out shopping with disposable cameras, and then used the resulting images as the foundation for a focus group conversation about the girls' experiences as consumers. Among the justifications Russell and Tyler offer for this research method is that youth-produced photographic images give the 'children the time and space in which to reflect on their own experiences and interpretations of the social world' (230), by framing the conversation around what the girls themselves found meaningful. The authors explore how these girls engage with consumer objects and physical spaces during their shopping expeditions, objects and spaces that hold meaning in the transition from childhood to adulthood: 'the management and commercialization of transitional objects, practices and spaces appears to be significant to the ways in which young girls experience the transition from childhood to young adulthood in a gendered way' (234).

Key points: Selected research on the impact of Disney on gender and intersecting inequalities

Given their global popularity as media products aimed at children, Disney films, videos, books and merchandise have received considerable scholarly attention, as the following examples illustrate.

- Hurley (2005) explores the impact of six Disney fairytales, comparing the original source texts with how the tales are told in a book marketed by Disney and in Disney films. Hurley focuses particularly on implications of images and content for the self-image of children of colour, arguing that the images and content are 'laced with White privileging' and 'with a binary color symbolism that associates white with goodness and black with evil' (229). She goes on to contend that the relative absence of positive portrayals of non-white and non-Western people has a negative impact: 'the damaging effects of the preponderance of the almost-all White world of the fairy tales, and particularly the fairy tale princess, should not be underestimated' (228).
- Lacroix (2004) also explores the intersections of race/ethnicity and gender in Disney films. She contends that 'The White heroine is largely asexual, focused on romance and marriage, is demure, although her world tolerates a contained rambunctiousness or rebellion' while female characters of colour are 'orientalised', and represented as 'sexualized beings, whose bodies are privileged as the sites of their power and agency' (227).
- Drawing on analysis of the films themselves and interviews with 5- to 8-year-old Korean immigrant girls in the United States, Lee (2008) finds that the girls largely accept the greater power Disney princes have in negotiating marriage relative to princesses. Though she considers the girls' responses to the films in the context of Korean cultural expectations (which are discussed more fully in the next section), she also finds that the girls largely view the gender inequity in which princes are the more powerful agents in deciding when and whom to marry as representative of general expectations in the United States overall.

Across national contexts, and with variations by race/ethnicity, class and culture, the scholars discussed so far document both change and continuing stereotypical media content. Though the change is crucial to keep in mind, so too is the continuing over-representation of boys and men, especially white boys and men, particularly in terms of roles that express power, activity and strength. But an exclusive focus on media content and its potential impact on children implies that children passively absorb whatever media messages surround them. Scholars, advocates and activists all recognize that is not the case, underscoring the importance of the next question.

How do children interpret, refine and resist media messages?

Media scholars emphasize the importance of agency, with the term 'audience reception' sometimes used to highlight the power of audiences to receive media messages in a wide variety of ways. This emphasis resonates with childhood studies, with its focus on children's active agency. Rysst (2010) explores how 10-year-old girls in Norway interpret their own clothing choices, 'studying children as active agents and from their point of view' (78). She spent 2 years as an ethnographer, observing children at two schools and also accompanying them to various sites, including shopping trips. Of particular interest to her is a generation gap in the interpretation of these young girls' clothing preferences: adults and even their teenaged older sisters criticize their choices as 'too sexy' for their age while the 10 year olds themselves consider their clothing 'just fashionable and *kul*' (90). Rather than privileging the adult interpretation, Rysst reminds her readers that the children's interpretations are valid too, and should be incorporated into any full understanding of the meaning of children's merchandise. The ambivalence the girls express about wanting to wear 'fashionable, teenage-like clothes' while still appearing adequately innocent (as captured in her article's title, 'I am only ten years old') reflects, in her analysis, the presence of 'competing and conflicting femininities for 10-year-old girls starting to want independence from the world of childishness' (86).

Lee (2008) also emphasizes children's agency in her research on how Korean immigrant girls interpret Disney films. Though she concludes these girls are influenced by Western and particularly US norms surrounding gender and marriage, she also notes that Korean cultural values about family 'significantly influenced their points of view' (39). In particular, she argues that the 5- to 8-year-old girls interviewed in her study tended to view marriage as a family matter, with decisions about timing and the appropriateness of a given marriage partner involving one's entire family rather than being decisions for the individual alone. As she puts it, 'research should consider the diverse meanings of popular culture that can be derived from young children who have different socio-cultural experiences' (44). Family influences as mediators in how children interpret popular culture are addressed by Bragg and Buckingham (2004) as well. They studied UK family television viewing with attention to how sexualized content is received. They argue that such viewing time often becomes a site of struggle, in which young people 'far from passively accepted parental regulation and moralization' (453). Patterns within those struggles varied by gender of both parent and child. For example, some boys in the study reported resisting their mothers' attempts to control their access to or interpretations of sexualized media content, 'defin(ing) themselves in opposition to their mothers' endeavours, sometimes with the active collusion of their fathers' (453).

Dennis (2009, 2010) studies gay youth reception of mainstream media content in the United States. Exploring fan mail and fan-produced art, he illuminates the many ways in which LGBT or questioning youth interpret and refine heteronormative media. 'How do juveniles go about recognizing and acknowledging that they experience same-sex desire when they are told, over and over, a dozen times a day, that such experience is impossible, that only heterosexual desire exists? One important strategy involves 'queering' favorite mass media texts, finding hints of same-sex desire in characters who are ostensibly heterosexual' (2010, 7). In the fan mail and fan art these youth often post online, they not only express their feelings of potential same-sex desire but also create virtual youth communities that offer peer support as they develop their sexual identity.

Examples of research: Two studies of alternative youth cultures

Skater girls

Kelly, Pomerantz and Currie (2005) interviewed Canadian girls who participate in skateboarding culture, delineating how they used this alternative culture to distance themselves from the mainstream culture of femininity that other scholars have termed 'emphasized femininity'. In the local context of the girls interviewed, emphasized femininity was identified with girls who 'spent their time shopping for fashionable, sexy clothing; applying makeup; flirting with boys; and talking about fashion and popular music' (245). The skater girls, on the other hand, 'produc(ed) themselves in relation to alternative images found, for example, among peers at school, at skate parks, on the streets, in songs and music videos, in skater magazines (online and in print), and so on.

Examples of research – Cont'd

The alternative authority of skater girl discourse gave the girls . . . room to maneuver within and against the culturally valued discourse of emphasized femininity' (245).

Emo gay boys

Peters (2010) draws on personal interviews, magazine articles and other cultural records (like photographs) to investigate how music and fashion are employed by gay boys who identify as 'emo' to define and shape a subculture. He describes the emo look as 'White, or at times vaguely Asian, with kittenish features, stick straight and dark hair, and milk white skin' (131). 'Its etymology comes from emotion(al), gesturing towards music and a lifestyle that prizes human emotions, structured through an aesthetic that emphasizes depth and seriousness' (132). Peters traces this phenomenon of the 1990s through to a more contemporary variation that is explicitly queer, marked by androgynous clothing and linked to a particular music scene, a 'distinction of emo' adopted by 'queer boys, between the ages of 14 and 22 (approximately) who are identifying with their homosexuality and who have adopted emo style to express their desires as an aesthetic that counters both gay and straight mainstream visions of (hyper)masculinity' (135).

Reflections on the research

Focusing on mainstream mass media may imply a homogeneous popular culture in which all children within a given geographic area internalize the same media messages and behave in very similar ways. The skater girls and the emo gay boys serve as reminders that many alternative subcultures exist, and youth are active agents in forming them, in part by drawing on alternative media and consumer goods like music, magazines and fashion. In both cases, though, they are in dialogue with more mainstream conceptions of femininity or masculinity too, conceptions they reject but cannot ignore.

Activity

Write a paragraph outlining how dominant conceptions of masculinity and femininity affect and shape the subcultures created by the skater girls and the emo gay boys, and addressing how the development of these subcultures demonstrates both the potential for, and limitations on, youth autonomy in relation to media messages.

Various scholars highlight the role teachers and child care providers can play in encouraging media literacy, helping children and youth raise critical questions about gender and sexuality-related messages in media content. For example, Chung (2007) 'provides art teachers with critical tools for educating (secondary students) about how hip-hop culture glorifies sexist portrayals' (33) while still respecting US youth attachment to this form of popular culture. Carrington and Hodgetts (2010) stress the increasing importance of virtual worlds in the media environment of children in the United Kingdom and Australia, arguing that the extensive amount of time children spend exploring those worlds online should be acknowledged. Focusing in particular on the gendered messages in a popular Barbie-themed virtual world website for young girls, they present evidence that children are visiting such worlds more often, and spending more significant periods of time when they visit. As a result, they call upon teachers to 'pay attention to the kinds of online and offline practices these worlds promote' (671).

Key points: Media activism

Along with the power to interpret and refine media products as individual consumers or loosely organized sub-cultural groups, youth also have the power to organize more formally – on their own or in partnership with adults – to resist mainstream media content and produce alternative media. The following list highlights just a few organizations around the world engaged in youth-relevant media activism that addresses gender and sexuality, listing the organization name, its web address and an excerpt from its website related to its mission and objectives.

- GLAAD, United States
  Mission: 'The Gay & Lesbian Alliance Against Defamation (GLAAD) amplifies the voice of the LGBT community by empowering real people to share their stories, holding the media accountable for the words and images they present, and helping grassroots organizations communicate effectively. By ensuring that the stories of LGBT people are heard through the media, GLAAD promotes understanding, increases acceptance, and advances equality'. Among its many projects, GLAAD helps LGBT youth 'share their stories in the media and better educate Americans about the need for LGBT-inclusive protections for young people' (www.glaad.org).
- Girls Making Media Project, Western Africa
  Objectives: 'To strengthen the capacity of . . . adolescent girls engaged in children and youth organizations from Ghana, Liberia, Sierra Leone and Togo to advocate against gender discrimination by making efficient use of diverse forms of media' as well as providing training for 'adult journalists in issues facing adolescent girls in West Africa' (www.plan-childrenmedia.org).
- Through the Gender Lens, Pakistan
  Objectives: This organization selected youth, both male and female, from throughout Pakistan for a year-long training program related to media and gender-based violence; youth 'were educated on what gender-based violence was, trained to deconstruct media messages (projections and stereotyping of women in the media as well as the manner in which gender-based crimes are reported) by monitoring a selected number of TV and radio programmes and print matter, and tasked to eventually produce gender-sensitive media content of their own' (www.newslinemagazine.com/2011/01/agents-of-change-youth-tackle-gender-based-violence).
- The Youth and Gender Media Project, United States
  Objectives: 'The Youth and Gender Media Project encompasses a growing collection of short films that capture the diversity and complexity of gender non-conforming youth . . . The films introduce radical new concepts for many audiences, from the very idea that a young child can be transgender and have the wherewithal to fight against the pressures to conform to a binary gender paradigm, to the new and still very rare use of hormone blockers to delay puberty (www.youthandgendermediaproject.org).

These activist projects seek to broaden gender and sexuality-based messages in media through the active participation of youth. Closing the chapter with these examples emphasizes that along with continuing limitations within media content, mass media also presents opportunities for youth agency in relation to gender and sexuality. Acknowledging children's voices and creativity highlights the possibilities for nuanced audience reception and significant social change, possibilities that appear more remote if the focus is only on media content.

Chapter activities

Activity 1: Intersectionality and media content

The diversity of children's gendered experiences by race/ethnicity, social class, nation, ability and other intersecting dimensions of inequality is a key theme of this book. Review the material included under the first key question of this chapter and list examples of variations in gender and sexuality-related media content by other dimensions of inequality. Then make another list of possible variations you think might merit consideration for those studies whose descriptions did not include specific mention of intersecting inequalities.

Activity 2: Media impact, resistance and agency

Agency and autonomy are key themes in childhood studies today, and this chapter has documented some of the ways these themes are evident in research and activism related to media. At the same time, many media researchers focus on media impact in a manner that implies children are shaped by media content in a relatively straightforward manner. Thinking about this tension between media as a powerful social force that shapes children's thinking 'from above' and children as active agents who interpret and even resist media content, consider which side of the tension you find more interesting and important for childhood studies.

Summary

This chapter has:

- Detailed the range of messages about gender and sexuality in childhood evident in media such as books, television, films, music, magazines, video games and internet content;
- Explored the impact of media messages on children, including their potential to reinforce and disrupt traditional approaches to gender and sexuality, as well as the possibilities for differential impacts based on intersecting inequalities;
- Highlighted the way children interpret, refine and resist media messages, including research on audience reception of media texts and the active formation of youth

subcultures that are developed in opposition to dominant media and marketing discourses;

- Spotlighted examples of gender and sexuality-related media activism, with organized groups advocating for greater media literacy among youth, strategic use of existing media to help youth communicate their perspectives and resources to help youth produce their own alternative media content.

Further reading

Davies, B. (1989), *Frogs and snails and feminist tales: Preschool children and gender*. Sydney, Australia: Allen & Unwin (2nd edn, 2003, Hampton Press).
Pioneering study, also referenced in Chapter 2, focused on how preschool children interpreted feminist fairy tales.
Gotz, M., Lemish, D., Aidman, A. and Moon, H. (2005), *Media and the make-believe worlds of children*. London, UK: Lawrence Erlbaum Associates.
With authors from Germany, South Korea, Israel and the United States, this book takes a global perspective on how media products affect children's fantasy worlds and the implications of those effects, including how girls and boys vary in their media-shaped fantasy worlds.
Robinson, K. H. and Davies, C. (2008), 'She's kickin' ass, that's what she's doing!' *Australian Feminist Studies*, 23, 57, 343–58.
Other studies in this chapter focus on media content produced for children. This study explores how childhood innocence versus agency is represented in films focused on young girls as central characters. The authors argue that these films offer a lens through which to 'critically examine relations between gender, sexuality, power and agency in children's lives' (343).

Research details

Songs, chants and children's sexual agency

Peer-reviewed journal. Izugbara (2005) draws on data from 'rural males ($N = 120$), ages ten through 21 in eight local villages in Obingwa area of Abia State, Nigeria' (58). The research methods include careful attention paid to building rapport with community leaders and parents in each village, as well as securing permission before interviewing children. Thirty-one different songs and chants were identified and transcribed.

Objectification of women in popular song lyrics

Peer-reviewed journal. Authors Bretthauer, Zimmerman and Banning (2006) conduct a qualitative content analysis of song lyrics from popular songs in the

United States. The songs were identified using the 'Hot 100' list generated by Billboard, a music marketing research service, thus documenting their wide distribution and popularity.

Star Wars and masculinities

Peer-reviewed journal. This article, by Bettis and Sternod (2009), relies on a research method common in communication studies, close-reading of specific cultural texts together with background research on fan reception of those texts and analysis of published cultural criticism.

Race, gender and media messages about beauty

Peer-reviewed journal. Gordon (2008) administered a survey to 176 African American girls in a single US secondary school. The average age of survey participants was 15, and they answered a series of questions about how much time they spend consuming various media products distributed primarily to Black audiences, the degree to which they identify with that media content and their attitudes about appearance and attractiveness.

Skater girls

Peer-reviewed journal. This analysis is based on 16 semi-structured interviews, each about an hour long, with a diverse group of 13- to 16-year-old girls who identified with skateboarding culture in and around the Canadian city of Vancouver. Kelly, Pomeranz and Currie's (2005) interview questions were designed to tease out what the girls 'say, do, wear, believe, value, and know that allows them to see themselves and be seen by others as skaters' (231).

Emo gay boys

Peer-reviewed journal. Peters (2010) bases his analysis on what he calls 'passive ethnography' (drawing on informal personal interviews and his own experiences in emo venues and various gay parties, bars and other gathering spots) as well as semiotic analysis, an approach in which cultural products (art, fashion, music) are analysed closely for signifiers, symbols and potential meanings.

Gender and Sexuality in Children's Peer Cultures 7

Introduction and key questions

Chapters 4–6 have explored family, education and media as social institutions in which children's gender and sexuality are constructed. Peer cultures have been noted as well, but in this chapter they receive more concentrated attention. This focus is an important one, given the emphasis on children's active agency within childhood studies and the centrality of interactional-level analysis to both childhood studies and gender studies. The chapter is organized around several key questions that highlight what scholars and activists have established about peer cultures as a site relevant to gender and sexuality in childhood:

- Why is it important to focus on children's peer cultures in understanding the social construction of gender and sexuality in childhood?
- How are gender and sexuality shaped within children's peer cultures?
- How do youth participate in more formal organizing and movements related to gender and sexuality?

Why is it important to focus on children's peer cultures in understanding the social construction of gender and sexuality in childhood?

This book began with a discussion of the emphasis within childhood studies on children as agents in their own lives, active forces who recreate and refine the social world rather than just passively accepting it as passed down by adults. In Chapter 2, this emphasis was linked to a shift in the literature in gender studies, with increasing attention focused on gender as actively created and recreated through complex interactive processes, rather than reliance on one-way socialization models that assume smooth internalization of gender roles. The intersection of those two emphases highlights children's autonomy, both as individuals and as active members of creative and dynamic peer cultures. As Thorne (1993) put it in her pioneering book on the social construction of gender in children's peer cultures: 'Of course children are strongly influenced by cultural beliefs and by parents, teachers, and other adults. But children's collective activities should weigh more fully in our overall understanding of gender and social life' (4).

A brief reminder of some of the studies already reviewed that document the significance of peer cultures is a good place to start. In Chapter 2, studies indicating the role of gender-differentiated peer play groups in reproducing gender differences in Brazil (Kosminsky and Daniel, 2005) and the association between gender nonconformity and social loneliness among Chinese children (Yu and Xie, 2010) both demonstrate the importance of peer cultures.

Table 7.1 highlights just a few more of the examples from around the world and across various age groups, from Chapters 4, 5 and 6.

The fact that these examples are drawn from the chapters on family, education and media respectively is a reminder that adult-led social institutions have the power to shape children's experiences but children also have power of their own within those arenas, and within the social worlds they create through

Table 7.1 Select examples of articles addressing the role of peer cultures in previous chapters

Author(s) and location	Specific topic	Role of peers/peer culture addressed	Presented in . . .
Karniol (2009), Israel	Influence of siblings on children's ideas about gender	5- to 6-year-old children with older siblings had more fixed ideas about gender, indicating that such ideas are generated in part by interaction with other children within the family	Chapter 4
McHale, Crouter and Whiteman (2003), USA	Influence of same-sex siblings on gender-typed behaviour of children	In this study, children with older siblings of the same sex were more gender-typed (for a variety of age groups)	Chapter 4
Jackson and Dempster (2009), UK	Role of school-based peer cultures in shaping boys' orientation towards education	Peer pressure within adolescent boys' social groups discouraged academic engagement, with masculinity defined within the peer group as requiring a detached attitude towards academic work	Chapter 5
Lamb and colleagues (2009), USA	Influence of peer interaction on discouraging sexist remarks	Once encouraged through teacher intervention, negative responses by peers to sexist remarks reduced their incidence and decreased gender-typing among primary school children	Chapter 5
Izugbara (2005), Nigeria	Songs and chants about sexuality in boys' peer cultures	Songs and chants performed among adolescent boys are an important site of agency but also tend to reinforce the subordination of women and girls	Chapter 6
Kelly, Pomerantz and Currie (2005), Canada	'Skater girl' peer cultures	Through creative reinterpretation of the expectations of traditional femininity, adolescent girls constructed an alternative 'skater girl' femininity for themselves	Chapter 6

daily interactions with their peers. Children are constrained by what adults surround them with. But children's agency and autonomy at the interactional level are critical to consider if we hope to understand how gender and sexuality are shaped and shifted throughout childhood.

How are gender and sexuality shaped within children's peer cultures?

A closer look inside children's peer cultures reveals a vibrant world in which social patterns are formed, tweaked and sometimes rearranged completely. Incorporating but also recasting the gender and sexuality-related messages around them, children are actively engaged in creating social norms in complex peer interactions. Their peer cultures are on display in many places, at many times, but one particularly common site for children to come together is – of course – at school. Rice, Merves and Srsic (2008), for example, document the school experiences of US girls with emotional and behavioural disabilities, finding that the larger number of boys than girls in most classrooms for students with these types of disabilities has important implications for the girls. With little same-sex peer support, the girls often feel isolated, and turn to either flirtatious or aggressive behaviours with boys in order to find a place for themselves in the peer group.

Example of research: Primary school 'studs'

Renold's (2007) observations and interviews in UK primary schools began with the assumption that children's peer cultures are a pivotal site for social analysis. As she puts it, children are 'active constructors and mediators of their social worlds and realities and worthy of study in their own right' (280). Renold explores how boys relate to the status of 'boyfriend', a status that was fraught during the late primary school years. It had the potential to mark the boys positively as heterosexual but also negatively as linked to girls and romance: 'boys were confronted with the paradox that being a boyfriend could be both masculinity confirming and masculinity denying' (293). Following three pre-teen boys as case studies, she documents three approaches to refining the position of boyfriend:

- *Narcissistic*: little emotional intimacy, dismissive treatment of girls, focus on sexual relationships with girls
- *Romantic*: emotionally intimate, focus on love and romance with girls, but combined with frequent assertion of masculine interests like sports

⇨

- *Platonic*: sensitive and easy-going friendships with girls, heterosexualized through minor physical activities like holding hands, which allowed friendships with girls to confirm rather than deny masculinity

All three approaches required careful negotiations during daily interactions within their male peer cultures to ensure the desired masculinity-confirming outcome. Though all three boys 'established themselves as the "studs" of the school . . . they drew upon the discourses of heterosexuality and invested in and capitalized on their dominant status and position of privilege as the stud of their class in very different ways, each producing different versions of a heterosexual masculinity' (285).

Reflections on the research

This study documents both a general pattern of emphasizing heterosexuality as well as variations among the boys in how they creatively negotiated multiple variations on heterosexual masculinity. Depending on the level of focus one applies, children's peer cultures usually include both some general patterns and some variations.

Activity

Thinking back to your own earlier school experiences or school-aged children you know, identify an example of a general pattern related to sexuality within a local peer culture and an example of sub-types or variations within that broader pattern.

Key points: Gender and sexuality in children's everyday peer interactions

Along with heteronormativity, children construct and enforce a variety of other gendered expectations in their everyday interactions with each other, as studies from across the globe reveal.

- *Appearance*: Bhana (2008) observed and interviewed 8- and 9-year-old South African boys, documenting the pressure they put on each other to valorize 'six packs and big muscles and stuff like that' even at an age much too young to achieve that appearance standard. Focusing on teenagers in the USA, Jones and Crawford (2006) studied over 400 boys and girls, concluding that both boys and girls reported appearance-related conversations with peers that made them feel pressured, and that boys 'perceived (even) more appearance pressure and teasing' (243). Their particular focus was on weight, with girls reporting peer pressure to maintain lower weights, while boys faced negative peer response if either overweight or underweight.
- *Play styles and conflict resolution*: Based on video-tapes of preschool classrooms in Turkey, Kyratzis and Tarim (2010) document how middle-class girls sanctioned one another if they deviated from egalitarian, cooperative play within their female peer group, but allowed more directive and hierarchical play when they played with boys. Boys in the age group 6–8 are the focus of Keddie's (2003) research in Australia, with her ethnographic study demonstrating that peer culture was 'particularly potent in shaping the boys' understandings of themselves and others', with the content of that understanding centred on 'physical domination, violence and aggression, and the denigration of females' (290).

⇨

> ## Key points – Cont'd
>
> - *Gendered attributes*: Reay (2001) studied peer group discourses among UK girls in a London primary school classroom, and found that through those discourses the girls constructed themselves as 'harder working, more mature, and more socially skilled' than the boys (153). Minks' (2008) exploration of singing games played by indigenous children in Nicaragua focuses on how the children use song to 'form and re-form' their identities, 'reshaping the forms and meanings of gender and sexuality' (36). Though she concludes that the games the children play often reproduce traditional expectations, including the expectation that boys will be bold while girls are more withdrawn, she also notes that the song games sometimes 'have the effect of unsettling clear gender divisions' (46).
> - *Academic interests*: In research on student interest in studying music, particularly singing, in the United Kingdom, Ashley (2010) concludes peers are a significant influence in discouraging boys, despite concerted efforts by teachers to include boys in music education. At the primary school level, she finds that girls discourage the boys, criticizing their participation. By secondary school, 'the male peer group becomes more critical whilst girls increasingly perceive boy singers as "cute"' (47). Girls are sometimes under-represented in higher-level math and science courses, and here too scholars have identified peer influences as one of many factors. For example, Parker and Rennie (2002) report that girls often face harassment or pressure from male peers in science and math classrooms. They present results from a programme designed to test how girls fare in single-sex math/science classrooms in both rural and urban Western Australia, concluding that the girls appreciated the lack of negative interactions with male peers in the girls-only classroom environment. (See Chapter 5 for more on controversies surrounding single-sex schooling.)

Gender segregation and gender-typing, though often evident in children's peer cultures, are not universal features of children's daily worlds, and researchers have focused on variations as well as the more general pattern of traditional gender differentiation. Kyratzis and Guo (2001), for instance, compare conflict resolution strategies within preschool peer groups in the United States and China, concluding that US boys tend to be more assertive than girls while in China this was less consistently the case. Pfaff's (2010) analysis of gender segregation in pre-adolescent peer groups in Germany documents how social class and gender intersect in peer cultures. Relying on quantitative data gathered over time, Pfaff shows that among children from upper-class families, peer groups become increasingly gender segregated with age, while children from lower social classes were more likely to remain in mixed-gender peer groups for longer. She argues that this variation is an important counterpoint to the 'two worlds hypothesis', which posits that children's largely gender-segregated peer interactions produce two very different worlds characterized by divergent styles. Though she acknowledges that difference as a broad pattern, she also notes important variations by culture, subgroup and situational context, with her focus on social class variations. Both situational variations and subgroup differences are addressed by Evaldsson (2003) in her analysis of foursquare games. Observing video-taped 'game play among girls and boys with immigrant backgrounds (Syrian, Kurdish, Chilean) from low-income families in a multiethnic school setting in Sweden', she argues that instead of consistent subordination and passivity, 'the girls (and boys) playfully mock challenged gender meanings such as boys' domination and girls' subordination' and that there was 'considerable variation in female physicality' (475). Though her primary focus is on the children's autonomous activity, Evaldsson also notes the potential role of adult influence and school policy in shaping children's peer interactions. 'The teachers' orientation towards gender equality/sameness and cross-sex activities and the availability of sports activities for girls outside school . . . helped the girls, with minority and lower working-class backgrounds, to develop physical skills, challenge boys' domination and employ power positions in games on the playground' (495).

Example of research: Public space, public policy and children's interactions

Studying playgrounds in multicultural neighbourhoods in Amsterdam, Karsten (2003) focuses on children's agency. Like Evaldsson, though, she also attends to the role of adults and public policy in shaping the context in which children develop their peer cultures. Her article begins with a series of questions: 'what can be said about gendered ways of playing, of using space and spending time? How does gender interact with other structuring principles such as ethnicity and class? How do children themselves confirm and contest gender divides? How do the design and equipment of particular playgrounds enter into the gender dynamics of play?' (458). The broader pattern documented by this research project was one of gender-segregated play in which boys' peer groups were larger and tended to dominate and control the physical space. But Karsten also reveals variations, with some girls challenging traditional gender divides, especially when their female peer groups were relatively large. Given that boys were more likely to engage in ball games and girls to use playground equipment like swings, slides and climbing structures, playgrounds with greater space allocated to that kind of equipment tended to attract a larger number of girls and allow them the larger peer groups that facilitated more challenges to traditional divides. That pattern leads Karsten to assert that the design of public playgrounds should include consideration of how they 'can serve both boys and girls equally' such that 'play opportunities may help children to cross rigid gender divides as and when they want' (471).

⇨

Example of research – Cont'd

Reflections on the research

Activity

Walk through a public playground or park where children are present, or think back to any playground or park you are familiar with from your past or work you currently do with children. Do you notice any patterns in terms of how boys and girls interact in both gender-segregated and gender-integrated groupings? Do you notice any variations by age or ethnicity? And how, if at all, do you think the physical layout of the space and equipment might shape the opportunities for gendered peer interactions? (If you walk through a public playground or park, do so just briefly and casually, as any formal observation of children at play may require explicit permission in order to be acceptable within the ethical guidelines of your college/university.)

Example of research: Policing and transgressing gender boundaries at camp

Researchers McGuffey and Rich (1999) analysed how 5- to 12 year-old boys and girls interact at a summer day camp in the United States.

- Drawing on the concept of hegemonic masculinity (introduced in previous chapters), they attend to 'how hegemonic masculinity is manifest in middle childhood play and used to re-create a gender order among children wherein the larger social relations of men's dominance are learned, employed, reinforced, and potentially changed' (609).
- 'Since boys and girls tend to organize themselves into gender-homogeneous groups, they are generally aware that their sphere of 'gender-appropriate' activities has boundaries. When they transgress these bounds, they enter a contested area that we refer to as the 'gender transgression zone' . . . it is in the GTZ that we should expect to find continuities, as well as changes, in the construction of 'gendered' activities and thus the definition of what is hegemonically masculine' (610).
- The authors conclude that it is only the highest status boys (defined primarily by athletic ability and successful enactment of hegemonic masculinity) who were able to redefine gender boundaries when they wish to do so, because their masculinity is not in question. These boys could, for example, engage in hand-clapping games normally associated only with girls while still being viewed as appropriately masculine. If lower-status boys entered the GTZ, their masculinity was questioned and their behaviour negatively sanctioned by peers. Thus, even when gender boundaries were crossed, the authors argue that they were ultimately maintained and even reinforced.

Reflections on the research

Activity

Identify a peer who attended camp as a child, or who has worked as a camp counsellor, in a setting that included boys. Describe McGuffey and Rich's basic findings to them; ask if they think similar patterns were evident in their own camp experiences, and if not, why they think their particular camp context may have been different from what the authors documented.

Interview with C. Shawn McGuffey about his research on peer cultures and parental influence

C. Shawn McGuffey is Associate Professor of Sociology and African and African Diaspora Studies at Boston College, United States. His current projects include the work on parental responses to child sexual abuse addressed in Chapter 4 and a project investigating the social psychology of Black rape survivors in the United States, Ghana and South Africa.

Emily Kane:	What surprised you the most about the process of conducting this particular research project or about the results?
C. Shawn McGuffey:	The results of the GTZ were based off my college senior thesis and, due to the fact that this was my first empirical study on the impact of gender, race and class, almost everything surprised me. It is one thing to read about the ways in which inequalities impact everyday life and quite another to systematically document, and critically analyse, those inequities in the lives of kids to whom you have become attached. What surprised me most, however, is how race and class impacted the lives of these boys and girls in very distinct ways. The boys were highly integrated – in terms of both daily interaction and in status. The girls, however, clearly separated on both class and racial lines. Girls only crossed class and racial lines when a boy threatened a girl or when a girl beat a boy in a game or sporting event. When a girl was threatened or teased by boys other girls usually went out of their way to protect the targeted girl. And when a girl out performed a boy in an activity all girls rallied around her. It was a great show of solidarity.
Emily Kane:	The GTZ study highlights children's agency, while your research on sexual abuse (featured in Chapter 4) focuses more on the role of parents. Could you comment briefly on how, in your scholarship, you think about the balance between children's agency and adult influences as gender and sexuality are socially constructed throughout childhood?
C. Shawn McGuffey:	Children's agency and adult influences continually recreate, produce and change the meanings of gender and sexuality throughout childhood. Adults clearly have a strong impact. Adults often decide where a child lives, and their financial and social resources often dictate with whom a child *can* interact, *where* that child can go and to *which* cultural products, practices and resources a child will be exposed. All of these adult influences produce and provide the social structures and cultural apparatuses from which children make sense of gender and sexuality. Nevertheless, research has shown that peer groups, rather than parents, are often a better predictor of children's behaviour and long-term outcomes. This suggests that children's agency and peer interactions are key to gender and sexual development and, I would add, the racial enactments of their gendered and sexual lives. That is, children

reflect, organize and assess how others see them, weigh the cost and benefits of certain gendered behaviours and through this reflection they form their gendered selves. This gives children, and adults as well, the opportunity to conform or reject gendered and sexual norms over time and in particular situations. From this perspective, adults primarily provide the building blocks for gender and sexual development, but through interaction with peers and other social institutions children often decide how and what they will build.

Most of the examples so far focus on interactions that do not include overt conflict, but rather the emergence of group norms or the relatively non-coercive enforcement of those norms. But peer cultures also include the potential for more explicit harassment, bullying and violence linked to gender and sexuality. A brief review of some scholarship documenting those patterns is important to any comprehensive account of the role of peer cultures.

As the studies included in Table 7.2 and many others document, children's peer cultures include gender and sexuality-based aggression. This aggression can take various forms, from verbal harassment to physical abuse, sexual harassment to ostracism. Even if adult supervisors attempt to enforce a cooperative and accepting environment, children's active agency sometimes includes peer activity that reinforces hierarchies of power based on gender, gender conformity and sexual orientation. And these forms of power intersect with other

Table 7.2 Gender and sexuality-related bullying, harassment and violence in peer cultures

Author(s) and location	Age range and research method	Patterns identified
Leach (2003), Zimbabwe, Malawi and Ghana	Adolescents in secondary schools; qualitative observation and interviews with students	'The abusive behaviour of boys towards girls (and also towards younger or more vulnerable boys) in school is in part the product of a peer culture which stresses male competition and sexual prowess as part of the process of learning to "be a man"' (385)
Honkatukia, Nyqvist and Pösö (2007), Finland	12–17 year olds in residential child welfare institutions; focus group interviews	Boys' and girls' peer cultures within the institution, a setting in which the youth residents had previously experienced and perpetrated violence, reinforced 'belligerent masculinities, vulnerable femininity and negotiable violence in heterosexual relationships' (56)

Table 7.2 Continued

Author(s) and location	Age range and research method	Patterns identified
Currie, Kelly and Pomerantz (2007), Canada	11- to 16- year-old girls, semi-structured interviews	Through gossip and ostracism as forms of 'relational aggression', 'girls' bodies and self-presentations are under constant assessment by peers' (31); even the most 'popular' girls were subject to this assessment, which the authors consider evidence that the process is not individual but a peer-group level phenomenon
Robinson (2005), Australia	12- to 17-year-old boys in 14 different schools, in-depth interviews and focus groups	Fear of rejection within their same-sex peer culture encouraged boys to sexually harass girls 'as a means through which to maintain and regulate hierarchical power relationships, not just in relation to gender but how it intersects with other sites of power such as "race" and class' (19)
Ewing Lee and Troop-Gordon (2011), USA	Primary school boys and girls, average age 9 years, survey	Peer harassment led boys to decrease any gender non-conforming behaviour they might have engaged in if most of their friends were boys, but boys with many female friends were less affected by peer harassment

inequalities, intersections that must be addressed if efforts to reduce bullying and harassment are to be fully effective.

Example of research: Intersectionality and bullying

Daley, Solomon, Newman and Mishna (2007) document peer bulling of gay, lesbian, bisexual and transgendered youth in Canada, with a particular focus on intersectionality. A series of quotes from their work capture some of its key conclusions:

- 'The perspectives of professionals and peer youth advocates working in LGBT communities suggest the importance of an intersectional approach in conceptualizing and addressing bullying among LGBT youth. Simultaneous and interacting experiences of oppression – based on gender, race/ethnicity and newcomer/citizenship status – may result in differences in the forms and experiences of bullying, as well as differences in the availability of appropriate and effective support and intervention' (23).
- 'The importance of the intersection of sexual orientation and gender in experiences of peer victimization is evoked in key informants' identification of gay youth whose gender expression is more stereotypically feminine and transgender females (male-to-female) as more likely to be bullied compared to those youth whose gender presentations

⇨

Example of research – Cont'd

ostensibly conform to their sex or who are transgender males (female-to-male). This dynamic may be accounted for through a consideration of the role of homophobia in regulating masculinity' (23).

- 'Strategies which are narrow in focus may require LGBT youth to prioritize which experience (e.g., sexism, racism, homophobia or xenophobia) they put forward. This, in itself, is a form of violence in its negation of youth's lived experience' (24).
- 'Programs or interventions that, in effect, require LGBT youth to leave part of their experience and other aspects of their social identity at the door seem unlikely to provide effective responses to bullying' (26).

Reflections on the research

This research offers an important reminder that not only can bullying be based on a complex set of intersecting inequalities, with children and youth targeted on the basis of multiple identities, but also that victims' willingness to access services may depend upon how sensitive service providers are to intersectionality. Understanding these young people's experiences, and designing interventions to support them, cannot be accomplished well without an intersectional perspective.

Activity

Search the web for an anti-bullying program or initiative in your area that focuses on sexual orientation. Review its mission or overview to see if it includes any attention to intersecting forms of inequality, and consider what you find in relation to Daley and colleagues' argument that narrow strategies can 'negate youth's lived experience'.

How do youth participate in more formal organizing and movements related to gender and sexuality?

While children's peer cultures play out informally across a variety of arenas such as schools, neighbourhoods, summer camps and city parks, recognizing children's autonomy also requires attention to more formal organizations and movements related to gender and sexuality that actively engage youth. In these instances we see clear examples of children as agents revising and resisting inequalities, and making social change. Previous chapters have included reference to such movements and organizations, like Posner and Odede's NGO in Kenya and student-organized GSAs in secondary schools (both discussed in Chapter 5) as well as youth-produced media initiatives (considered in Chapter 6). This section highlights additional examples of the range of youth-powered initiatives around the world.

Many adult-led organizations prioritize the inclusion of youth as equal partners in their endeavours, offering youth key roles in defining the agenda and executing the work of gender and sexuality-related social change. UNICEF is a case in point. Their programmes include many that focus on gender equality in education, families and work, plus sexuality-related education. Throughout their initiatives around the world, they seek to recognize youth as active participants.

> Bursting with vitality, curiosity and spirit, young people have the potential to help advance the world . . . UNICEF works with and for adolescents to involve them in life-affirming activities. When they are appreciated as sources of energy, imagination and passion, young people flourish and so their communities flourish. (www.unicef.org/adolescence/index.html)

Following this UNICEF guideline, researchers in Bosnia and Herzegovina worked collaboratively with youth to study 'local understandings, needs, and actions about HIV/AIDS' (among other topics) in three localities (Maglajliá and Tiffany, 2006, 163). Youth researchers concluded that peer interactions and participatory peer education were the most effective sites at which to raise awareness and promote healthy behaviours (176). Though not UNICEF-funded, a similar approach was taken in Toronto, Canada, where an interdisciplinary team of researchers has been conducting a survey of teen sexual health. They invite local youth to participate as equal partners in the research process, from the earliest design stages developing the survey questionnaire through data collection, data analysis and implementation of policies suggested by the results. As Flicker and seven colleagues (2010) note: 'When given the chance, young people co-researching can take the research agenda in exciting new directions that reflect the realities of their unique social location and life circumstances' (136). The researchers in charge of the Toronto Teen Survey recognized that only through formal channels that treated youth as full partners could they ask the right questions, recruit an adequately diverse sample of survey participants, interpret their findings accurately and spread the word about what they had learned and its implications for policy and practice. Youth participants improved the research process and also became active peer educators on sexuality-related topics in their schools and communities.

These kinds of initiatives can build youth capacity for formal organizing and thus allow youth voices to have a real impact on public policy and other everyday outcomes related to gender and sexuality. But Maglajliá and Tiffany (2006) warn that this potential is not always realized: 'while youth participation is a 'hot' global and national issue, the emphasis on involving young people has too often resulted in little or no benefit to the lives of ordinary youth' (179). Based on their experience in Bosnia and Herzegovina, they recommend that groups seeking to respect youth agency and autonomy pay careful attention to 'transforming power relationships' between NGOs and government groups, their adult leaders and youth (180). Caribbean activist and lecturer Hosein (2007) offers a related argument about youth activism in Trinidad and Tobago. Though she explains that youth have organized to promote sexual and reproductive health, she also notes that their organizations are often 'partly dependent on international or state funding' (127). She believes this dependence shapes the issues youth pursue in their activist work, directing them towards a somewhat narrow focus. Instead of connecting sexual and reproductive health questions to broader structures of gender inequality and economic justice, Hosein argues that youth movements are encouraged to define those questions at the individual-level and address them through increased availability of social and health care services. 'Largely, the movement's approach has been to mediate, help people cope and reform policy and legislation, rather than to advocate for, or create, alternatives' (129). Though these goals are positive ones, she believes that without their dependence on international NGOs and the national government for funding, youth could more effectively 'move beyond a discourse about individual practice to one of equity and human rights' (127).

Hierarchies of power and access to political influence make it uncommon for youth movements or initiatives to be entirely independent of adult funding and direction, but some examples point to even greater youth autonomy in gender and sexuality-related organizing. GSAs in secondary schools in the United States emerged from youth protest, and though some teacher support was necessary for their development, many remain largely student-led, with a strong focus on shifting peer cultures to make schools more accepting of a range of gender and sexual identities.

Example of research: Queer youth activism in urban schools

In a critical review of scholarly literature on the experiences of lesbian, gay, bisexual, transgender and questioning youth in urban schools in the United States, Blackburn and McCready (2009) stress youth agency by identifying student activism as an important theme. Like many scholars, activists and advocates working on LGBTQ issues, they refer to members of this community as queer, an inclusive term that makes room for many varieties of gender and sexuality-based expression. The authors detail three types of queer student activism most evident across the research literature: students initiating and leading professional development trainings for their schools' administrators and teachers; students introducing new materials into their schools' curricula by providing them to teachers or directly to peers in class; and GSAs. In terms of GSAs, the authors note both successes and the need for continued refinement of the model. 'GSAs hold tremendous promise as organizations that support the development of queer youth in schools . . . However, there is a growing number of studies of GSAs that suggest that queer youth who attend urban schools in non-White, multiracial, poor, and working class communities experience difficulty starting and/or accessing their schools' GSAs' (226). Like Daley and colleagues' Canadian study of anti-bullying programmes, noted in a previous research example, this study concludes with a call for adult advocates to attend to intersectionality. 'Urban educators working with queer youth need to understand and be prepared to address multiple social and cultural issues that intersect with sexual and gender identities. This necessitates an intersectional analysis' (229).

Reflections on the research

Even in this brief summary, you can find language that suggests youth agency and autonomy as well as language that suggests adults (teachers and administrators) or schools as organizations are responsible for shaping the experiences of youth.

Activity

Re-read the summary, and take note of phrases that you think highlight youth agency versus adult responsibility. How do you think adult and child/youth involvement can best be balanced in creating more inclusive climates within schools? What tensions do you think are likely to arise between adults and children/youth in schools as that balance is established?

From GSAs in schools to community outreach related to sexual health, youth–adult partnerships and more fully youth-led organizations and movements document that children's peer worlds can be a site of resistance to traditional expectations and a positive source of social change.

Key points: Youth participation in formal organizations and initiatives

A few more examples help demonstrate the range of work that youth come together to pursue, shaping their own social worlds to include greater equality in relation to gender, sexuality and intersecting forms of inequality.

- In an in-depth analysis of teenage girls' activism that includes groups in Venezuela, Argentina, Mexico, United States and Canada, Taft (2010) documents many specific causes, some of which relate to gender and sexuality (fighting gender-based violence, advocating for LGBT rights and working against hate crimes based on intersecting inequalities). Across the various groups and causes she studied, Taft finds that whether their specific focus is on gender and sexuality-related social change or not, being activists gives teenage girls 'a way of being in the world that is different from that suggested by conventional gender roles and the pressures of emphasized femininity' (83).
- The *GSA Network*, a US organization, sponsors what it calls GSA Activist Camps: 'youth-planned, youth-led summer training academies' for students involved in GSAs at their schools, with the goal of further enhancing the leadership and activism capacities of those students and a focus on 'the ways that homophobia and transphobia are connected to racism, sexism, classism and other oppressions' (www.gsanetwork.org/events/activist-camps).
- Seventeen-year-old Brazilian activist Brisa De Angulo founded the *Centro Una Brisa de Esperanza* (CUBE), an organization dedicated to combating child and adolescent sexual abuse. 'CUBE started as an NGO where victims of sexual abuse could come to have someone who listened, but CUBE rapidly grew into a centre offering legal, social, and psychology support. It has become a centre where each child and adolescent victim receives comprehensive assistance and is provided a support system' (www.abreezeofhope.org).
- Philippine youth activist John Montilla has won international awards for the work of his NGO *Kabataang Gabay sa Positibong Pamumuhay* (KGPP). The group works with urban street youth to address the health impacts of sexual exploitation, through social entrepreneurship programmes that help youth develop and market products and become self-supporting. More information about Montilla's organization is available on the website Taking it Global, which describes itself as 'the largest online community of youth interested in global issues and creating positive change' (www.tigweb.org/).

Children's agency has been a theme throughout this book, but the detailed examples considered in this chapter establish even more explicitly the importance of peer cultures in shaping childhood gender and sexuality. Children's own social worlds and everyday interactions with each other play a crucial role in potentially reproducing, but also resisting and reshaping, traditional expectations related to gender and sexuality. Through formal advocacy and activism, children and youth also take part in organized political and social change work, forging peer cultures oriented towards loosening the constraints imposed by gender, sexuality and intersecting inequalities.

Chapter activities

Activity 1: Individual level and interactional level influences

Chapter 2 included a discussion of the idea that gender is socially constructed at the individual, interactional and institutional levels. While some people might assume that children's gender-typical behaviour is a reflection of their individual-level preferences, attention to peer cultures reveals that sometimes interactions with peers pushes children to fulfil gender expectations even if they do not personally prefer to do so. Pick an example of such an influence from this chapter, and think about how you might design an intervention to reduce peer pressure at the interactional level in relation to this particular example while still respecting children's agency.

Activity 2: Youth autonomy and adult support

Several examples in this chapter raised the question of how much power and autonomy youth have to organize in resistance to gender and sexuality-related constraints. Visit the Taking it Global website and go to their tool for searching organizations, at www.tigweb.org/resources/orgs/index.html. Search for groups addressing topics related to gender (there is a keyword search available on the page). For the organizations that come up, select a couple in regions of the world of particular interest to you, and review their overviews (or visit their home sites) to determine how you think youth and adults share leadership of the organizations. To what extent do you think youth autonomy is reflected in the organizations' mission, leadership and approach?

Summary

This chapter has:

- Reviewed a range of research studies documenting the importance of peer cultures in the social construction of gender and sexuality in childhood, at sites from schools to families to camps, neighbourhoods, parks and street cultures;
- Explored the agency of children and youth as social actors, as they reproduce gendered outcomes through routine everyday interactions as well as more dramatic instances of harassment and violence, but also as they refine and resist traditional gender expectations;
- Considered the balance between children's autonomy within their peer cultures and the constraints created by adult-led social institutions/public policy and individual adults such as parents, teachers and human services professionals, all in the context of the constraints children face from intersecting inequalities;

- Presented brief summaries of youth participation in more formal organizations, initiatives and movements seeking to loosen the constraints of gender and sexuality-based social expectations around the world.

Further reading

Bhana, D., Nzimakwe, T. and Nzimakwe, P. (2011), 'Gender in the early years: Boys and girls in an African working class primary school', *International Journal of Educational Development*, 31, 5, 443–8.

Argues that for teacher interventions aimed at gender equity to be effective, teachers must acknowledge young children 'as agents of gender and sexuality' and 'acquaint themselves with emerging theories and research around gender and childhood studies' (446).

Fingerson, L. (2006), 'Agency and the body in adolescent menstrual talk', *Childhood*, 12, 1, 91–110.

Through individual and group interviews, US researcher Fingerson documents how adolescent girls 'collectively construct menstruation and the body in creative ways', resisting negative framings of themselves and 'exert(ing) agency in their negotiations with the gendered world and social structure' (91).

Rosario, M., Schrimshaw, E. and Hunter, J. (2004), 'Ethnic/racial differences in the coming-out processes of lesbian, gay, and bisexual youths', *Cultural Diversity and Ethnic Minority Psychology*, 10, 3, 215–28.

Concludes that US Black and Latino youths are less likely to be connected to LGBT peers and/or gay and lesbian social and cultural activities, due to pressures from within their racial/ethnic communities.

Research details

Primary school 'studs'

Peer-reviewed journal. Renold (2007) spent a year conducting an ethnographic study of about 60 children in two primary schools in 'a small semi-rural town in the east of England', 'exploring the construction of children's gender and sexual identities in their final years (year 6) of primary school' (279). Most were from 'white, working- and middle-class families' (279).

Public space, public policy and children's interactions

Peer-reviewed journal. Karsten (2003) worked with a research team to observe eight public playgrounds in Amsterdam, each situated in a different multicultural neighbourhood, over a two-month period in early summer. These locations were selected to offer a range of size and equipment quality, plus variation in neighbourhood demographics. 'During the intensive fieldwork we used different methods: informal and structured observations, countings and interviews' (463), as well as spatial mappings of the physical space.

Policing and transgressing gender boundaries at camp

Peer-reviewed journal. McGuffey spent 315 hours over a nine week period as a participant observer (both a camp counselor and researcher) in a US day camp. Then McGuffey and his co-author Rich (1999) analysed the observational data. The campers included both boys and girls from a diverse array of social class and racial/ethnic backgrounds. McGuffey also 'interviewed 22 of the children and 6 parents near the end of the summer' (611).

Intersectionality and bullying

Peer-reviewed journal. Daley and colleagues (2007) used what social science researchers call purposive sampling (carefully selecting participants based on the knowledge and expertise they bring to a given research question) to 'identify individuals representing diverse roles and settings with expertise on LGBT youth' (13). Their interviewees included nine key informants: four female, four male and one transgendered. Their racial/ethnic backgrounds and sexual orientations varied, as did their work settings (e.g. schools, social services agencies).

Queer youth activism in urban schools

Peer-reviewed journal. Blackburn and McCready (2009) conducted a careful review of the existing scholarship by other researchers to determine themes that emerge. They focus mostly on qualitative research studies from the United States, all based in urban schools. As they put it, 'our purpose is to listen to voices presented in multiple and variable texts to figure out how context matters' (223).

8 Conclusion

Introduction and key questions

Pulling together themes, approaches and findings presented in the previous chapters, this conclusion answers three key questions:

- What does research suggest as key issues in rethinking gender and sexuality in childhood?
- What does research document as promising avenues for social change?
- How are advocates and activists working to increase equality and address children's rights in relation to gender and sexuality?

What does research suggest as key issues in rethinking gender and sexuality in childhood?

Introduced in Chapters 1 and 2, and then woven into the exploration of specific findings presented in Chapters 3–7, is a series of key themes and issues that scholars consider crucial to understanding childhood gender and sexuality. Those working in childhood studies emphasize childhood as socially constructed; children's agency, autonomy and rights; the importance of children's voices; and recognizing inequalities among children by race/ethnicity, nationality, gender, sexual orientation, religion, ability/disability and economic class. Gender studies scholars often highlight an overlapping set of themes: the social construction of gender and sexuality at multiple levels (individual, interactional, institutional); the continuum of gender and sexual identities that goes far beyond simple binaries of male/female and heterosexual/gay; the intersection of gender/sexuality with other inequalities like the ones increasingly addressed within childhood studies; and the importance of addressing not only girls but also boys in the study of gender. Together, these two sets of trends intersect in the growing and vibrant scholarly literature on gender and sexuality in childhood. Balancing attention to structural and institutional constraints as well as children's agency and autonomy, and doing so with nuanced recognition of cross-cutting inequalities both across and within nations, researchers interested in children's gender and sexuality are listening to children's voices, exploring their everyday peer worlds and avoiding fixed assumptions about both childhood and gender/sexuality. As Davies put it in her author interview, included in Chapter 2: 'I think of research – and indeed any meeting with children – in terms of an encounter where each is open to the other and is open to being moved by the other'. A pioneer in expanding our view of gender and sexuality in childhood by looking at things from children's perspectives and questioning rather than assuming binary gender categories, Davies helped to forge a path that is now crowded with exciting research and activism of the sort described throughout this book. And that work clearly documents how gender and sexuality are constructed, resisted, reshaped and revised in families, schools, media and children's peer cultures, with active roles played by children themselves, as well as parents, relatives, siblings, teachers, school administrators, doctors, social service professionals, media producers, child advocates and activists, lawyers, politicians and policymakers across the globe. A wealth of research findings and activist initiatives, policy agendas and organizations both large and small, have been reviewed, offering a primer that hopefully encourages readers to dig deeper on their own, and explore even more of the vast array of work taking place around the world.

What does research document as promising avenues for social change?

Social change has been presented as a major theme in this volume, as has the importance of research and scholarship in shaping policies, initiatives and interventions. Therefore, the conclusion is a good place to step back and emphasize again the possibilities for change, possibilities that respect the agency of children and youth, and seek to expand their rights and opportunities in relation to gender and sexuality.

Key points: Selected examples of social change advocacy

Even reviewing a few examples from each of the previous chapters makes it clear that researchers, activists, policymakers, children's advocates and children themselves are actively engaged in rethinking gender and sexuality, with scholarship helping to direct, evaluate and refine many initiatives. Organized by chapter, this brief list highlights just a few selected previous examples related to family, education, media and peer cultures, but more are included within those chapters.

- *Family*: In Trinidad and Tobago, government-funded programmes have helped parents learn new approaches to communicating with their adolescent children about sexuality and sexual health, and research has documented the impact of those programmes (Baptiste and colleagues, 2009); in the United States, scholars have argued that a child-centred approach to domestic violence research can help practitioners design more effective programs to reduce gendered violence among adolescents (Phillips and Phillips, 2010); and in the UK, researchers have entered policy debates to present evidence that the lack of same-sex role models has no negative effect on children's gendered identities in gay and lesbian families (Clarke and Kitzinger, 2005; Hicks 2008).
- *Education*: In Tanzania, researchers have provided evidence of progress in the expansion of secondary school opportunities for girls (Okkolin, Lehtomäki and Bhalalusesa 2010); Lamb and colleagues' (2009) US study established the effectiveness of a school-based intervention programme in encouraging primary school students to confront

sexist remarks from peers; and Edstrom (2009) explores the impact of state policy in fostering gender equity at the preschool level in Sweden and Scotland.

- *Media*: Along with attention to the ways in which youth actively interpret and develop media content that expands gender and sexuality-based constraints, educational researchers have urged teachers to implement media literacy curricula that respect children's media interests while also fostering their capacity for critical reflection on media content. US researcher Chung's (2007) suggestions for helping students critically analyse hip-hop culture's gender portrayals and UK and Australian scholars Carrington and Hodgetts' (2010) call for teachers to attend to the gender messages in the online virtual worlds their students inhabit are two examples.

- *Peer Cultures*: Canadian researchers document that attention to and connection with youth peer cultures improves sexual health research and intervention practices (Flicker and colleagues, 2010); US scholars review evidence that student-run gay–straight alliances can notably improve the climate for students of all genders and sexualities in schools (Blackburn and McCready, 2009); Dutch researcher Karsten (2003) reminds policymakers and space planners that research findings can help in designing playground facilities that foster positive peer interactions among and between boys and girls.

The work of researchers has been a central focus of this book, and brought to life not only the many examples of research and citations included but also the author interviews that appear in select chapters. Some of those authors referred specifically in their interviews to the implications their research has for policy or interventions. A few quotes help to illuminate further the connections between scholarship influenced by the new childhood studies and social change initiatives related to childhood gender and sexuality.

Key points: Interviewed authors on links between research featuring children's voices and social change

- Heather Montgomery, profiled in Chapter 4: 'The obvious response when child prostitution is found is to go in with all guns blazing, arrest the men, rehabilitate the children and remove them from their parents. But this was just what the children feared. They did not want to see their parents punished in any way. In 1996 the law was changed in Thailand to enable the prosecution of parents who allowed or encouraged their children to work as prostitutes. Given the emphasis the children placed on family relationships and filial obligations, such laws would make it extremely difficult for the children to ask for help, even if they recognised they needed it. Keeping the family together was their primary justification for what they did, the prosecution and imprisonment of their parents their worst fear . . . therefore I think it is important to conduct small scale ethnographic research and to use that to build up a holistic picture of children's lives, their needs and their own desires'.

⇨

> ## Key points – Cont'd
>
> - Deevia Bhana, profiled in Chapter 5: 'In relation to teenage sexuality, my work high-lights the ways in which young people actively aspire towards relationships based on love . . . but they note how little they can talk about these matters in Life Orientation courses in schools. A major intervention in this regard is to ensure that the actual lives and identities and pleasures and dangers of young people feature as a necessity in sexuality education programmes'.

Many other scholars featured throughout this book are committed to seeing their research inform policies and practices that impact the lives of children and youth and expand or incorporate their agency. Along with the quotes offered from previously interviewed authors, the next box presents a new interview to explore further the ways researchers are contributing to social change.

Interview with Peter Newman about his research on LGBTQ youth

Peter Newman is Professor at the University of Toronto's Factor-Inwentash Faculty of Social Work and also holds the Canada Research Chair in Health and Social Justice. His primary research is on HIV prevention and global health, with a focus on social and structural factors that produce risk. His work on LGBT youth includes the research presented in Chapter 7, as well as work on how the discourse of 'conversion', and discredited attempts to 'change' gay people to straight, enable and promote bullying of LGBT youth.

Emily Kane:	One of this book's themes is the potential of research and scholar-ship to contribute to policy/practice related to childhood gender and sexuality. How do you see your co-authored work on bullying and LGBT youth (featured in Chapter 7) as having that potential?
Peter Newman:	Particularly in the field of social work, with its strong applied focus, we aim to use research to inform individual practitioners, social service agencies, social policies and the larger discourse on bullying to recognize the ways in which homophobic bullying is both similar to and distinct from general bullying of youth. For one, it's impor-tant to specifically name anti-gay bullying; it's often overlooked, which drives LGBT youth further underground. Often schools and parents do not intervene effectively, if at all. Some of the major social institutions that impact on youths' lives – schools, organized religion, sports – themselves harbour and even promote anti-LGBT attitudes; thus what may be part of the solution for heterosexual youth is often part of the problem for LGBT youth. Using research to help practitioners, agencies, policymakers and the public identify

and intervene against homophobic bullying has important potential for advancing policy and practice, and thus improving the lives of LGBT youth.

Emily Kane: Another key theme is the importance of children's agency and voice. How does recognition of youth agency shape your approach to research and advocacy?

Peter Newman: The very recognition of intersectionalities supports youth's agency in opening up the field for self-definition. Some youth talk about the primacy of the challenge of not knowing why they are targeted. Is it because I'm black? Because I'm female? Because I'm a lesbian? Some find that more concerning than the harassment itself. Intersectionalities may open up space for youth to work through their multiple and dynamic identities. Another important construct is youth's competence and resilience. We've identified an array of responses among LGBT youth to being bullied, many of which are empowering; and most LGBT young people survive and thrive, even amidst the challenges of a sometimes hostile social environment.

How are advocates and activists working to increase equality and address children's rights in relation to gender and sexuality?

Some researchers are directly involved in social change work, while others contribute to scholarly literature that indirectly shapes the context within which social change initiatives are forged. Whether they are researchers as well or not, advocates and activists – including youth activists – have been featured throughout. As this book comes to a close, a spotlight on the kinds of organizations and initiatives that seek to increase equality and expand children's rights in relation to gender and sexuality is a fitting place to end. Table 8.1 draws together just a few selected examples from across previous chapters.

The range of activity could fill volumes. The Canada-based White Ribbon Campaign (www.whiteribbon.com/international) has sparked initiatives in 60 different nations that include male youth engagement in combating violence against girls and women. Gender Spectrum (www.genderspectrum. org) is a US organization advocating for families with 'children who don't fit neatly into male and female boxes'. The European Union's 'Youth Strategy'

Table 8.1 Selected examples of organizations and initiatives from previous chapters

Organization and location	Focus and mission	Presented in . . .
Gender Identity Research and Education Society, UK	Advocates for transgender individuals and their families, including focus on youth issues	Chapter 3
UNICEF, International	Gender-sensitive programming related to youth education, sexual and reproductive health and protection from abuse	Chapter 3
Centre for Studies and Applied Sciences in Gender, Family, Women and Adolescents (CSAGA), Vietnam	Programmes include child abuse protection advocacy that is attentive to gendered violence within families	Chapter 4
Shining Hope for Communities, Kenya	Advocates for educational access and quality for girls	Chapter 5
Through the Gender Lens, Pakistan	Youth media literacy and alternative media production project aimed at developing youth-produced content to reduce gendered violence	Chapter 6
Gay–Straight Alliance Network, USA	Resources and collaboration opportunities for youth-led GSAs from across the USA	Chapter 7

(ec.europa.eu/youth) for 2010–18 includes the collection and distribution of youth statistical indicators on gender equity in education, poverty and housing. The Progressive Organization of Gays in the Philippines, or PROGAY (http://progay.multiply.com), is working for gay rights in the Philippines, including legislative initiatives to fight discrimination affecting gay students in schools. With recognition of children's agency, autonomy and rights, plus recognition of the limitations imposed by traditional expectations and the importance of acknowledging diversity, a multitude of initiatives, organizations and policy efforts around the world are pushing to help children and youth expand their options and opportunities in terms of gender and sexuality. Scholarship in childhood studies, gender studies, education, psychology, sociology, anthropology and numerous other fields demonstrates the patterns of inequality affecting children and youth. But it also documents the potential for social change and active agency. In complex ways that vary by nation and region, religion, social class, racial and ethnic identity, physical and mental ability/disability, with the support of governments and NGOs or in opposition to them, youth and their advocates are successfully carving out new possibilities, and rethinking conventional wisdom about gender and sexuality in childhood.

Chapter activities

Activity 1: Diversity in childhood gender and sexuality

An important theme throughout this book has been the diversity of experiences and tensions that characterize childhood gender and sexuality when we attend to variations by economic class, race/ethnicity, ability/disability, nation, religion and other dimensions of variation in childhood. Pick a region of the world, and review the preceding chapters looking for examples of research from that region. How many of these appear to attend to diversity within the region/nation on which they focus?

Activity 2: Children's voices and social change

From among Chapters 4–7, which address family, education, media and peer cultures respectively, select one of particular interest to you. Reviewing that chapter, list at least six research studies mentioned and note for each to what extent it seems to include children's voices in the research design. Then, for each, jot down a few notes on how the author(s) might further incorporate children's voices and acknowledge their agency/autonomy. Finally, after re-reading this chapter's author interview quotes about children's voice in research and social change, consider what implications you think the presence or absence of children's voices in these studies has for the ability of the research to effectively inform social change initiatives related to gender or sexuality in childhood.

Summary

This chapter has:

- Revisited selected examples of scholarship and activism from previous chapters in order to highlight key themes of the book;
- Emphasized the importance of research and children's voices in informing advocacy and social change in relation to gender and sexuality-based limitations affecting children and youth;
- Underscored the wide range of advocacy initiatives from around the world that seek to broaden and rethink those limitations.

References

Adely, F. J. (2007), 'Is music haram?: Jordanian girls educating each other about nation, faith, and gender in school', *Teachers College Record*, 109, 7, 1663–81.

Aghajanian, A., Tashakkori, A., Thompson, V., Mehryar, A. H. and Kazemipour, S. (2007), 'Attitudes of Iranian female adolescents toward education and nonfamilial roles', *Marriage & Family Review*, 42, 1, 49–64.

Ahmed, S., Morrison, S. and Hughes, I. (2004), 'Intersex and gender assignment: The third way?' *Archives of Disease in Childhood*, 89, 9, 847–50.

Ali, Z., Fazil, Q., Bywaters, P., Wallace, L. and Singh, G. (2001), 'Disability, ethnicity, and childhood', *Disability and Society*, 16, 949–68.

Al-Shehab, A. J. (2008), 'Gender and racial representation in children's television programming in Kuwait', *Social Behavior & Personality: An International Journal*, 36, 1, 49–63.

Anderson, E. (2002), 'Openly gay athletes: Contesting hegemonic masculinity in a homophobic environment', *Gender & Society*, 16, 6, 860–77.

Ashley, M. (2010), 'Slappers who gouge your eyes: Vocal performance as exemplification of disturbing inertia in gender equality', *Gender and Education*, 22, 1, 47–62.

Baird, A. L. and Grieve, F. G. (2006), 'Exposure to male models in advertisements leads to a decrease in men's body satisfaction', *North American Journal of Psychology*, 8, 1, 115–21.

Bajaj, M. (2009), 'Un/doing gender?: A case study of school policy and practice in Zambia', *International Review of Education*, 55, 5/6, 483–502.

Baker-Sperry, L. (2007), 'The production of meaning through peer interaction: Children and Walt Disney's Cinderella', *Sex Roles*, 56, 11/12, 717–27.

Baker-Sperry, L. and Grauerholz, L. (2003), 'The pervasiveness and persistence of the feminine beauty ideal in children's fairy tales', *Gender & Society*, 17, 5, 711–26.

Baptiste, D. R., Kapungu, C., Miller, S., Crown, L., Henry, D., Da Costa Martinez, D. and Jo-Bennett, K. (2009), 'Increasing parent involvement in youth HIV prevention: A randomized Caribbean study', *AIDS Education and Prevention*, 21, 6, 495–511.

Bayne, E. (2009), 'Gender pedagogy in Swedish preschools', *Gender Issues*, 26, 2, 130–40.

Beh, H. and Diamond, M. (2005), 'Ethical concerns related to treating gender nonconformity in childhood and adolescence: Lessons from the family court of Australia', *Health Matrix: Journal of Law-Medicine*, 15, 2, 239–83.

Bettie, J. (2002), 'Exceptions to the rule: Upwardly mobile white and Mexican American high school girls', *Gender & Society*, 16, 3, 403–22.

Bettis, P. and Sternod, B. (2009), 'Anakin Skywalker, Star Wars and the trouble with boys', *Thymos: Journal of Boyhood Studies*, 3, 1, 21–38.

Bhana, D. (2008), '"Six packs and big muscles, and stuff like that": Primary school-aged South African boys, black and white, on sport', *British Journal of Sociology of Education*, 29, 1, 3–14.

— (2009), '"They've got all the knowledge": HIV education, gender and sexuality in South African primary schools', *British Journal of Sociology of Education*, 30, 2, 165–77.

Bhana, D., Nzimakwe, T. and Nzimakwe, P. (2011), 'Gender in the early years: Boys and girls in an African working class primary school', *International Journal of Educational Development*, 31, 5, 443–8.

Bhat, B. A. (2010), 'Gender, education, and child labour', *Educational Research and Reviews*, 5, 6, 323–8.

Birdsall, N., Levine, R. and Ibrahim, A. (2005), 'Towards universal primary education: Investments, incentives, and institutions', *European Journal of Education*, 40, 337–49.

Birkett, M., Espelage, D. L. and Koenig, B. (2009), 'LGB and questioning students in schools: The moderating effects of homophobic bullying and school climate on negative outcomes', *Journal of Youth and Adolescence*, 38, 7, 989–1000.

Blackburn, M. and McCready, L. (2009), 'Voices of queer youth in urban schools', *Theory Into Practice*, 48, 3, 222–30.

Bos, H. and Sandfort, T. (2010), 'Children's gender identity in lesbian and heterosexual two-parent families', *Sex Roles*, 62, 1/2, 114–26.

Bragg, S. and Buckingham, D. (2004), 'Embarrassment, education, and erotics', *European Journal of Cultural Studies*, 7, 4, 441–59.

Bretthauer, B., Zimmerman, T. S. and Banning, J. H. (2006), 'A feminist analysis of popular music: Power over, objectification of, and violence against women', *Journal of Feminist Family Therapy*, 18, 4, 29–51.

Brison, K. J. (2009), 'Shifting conceptions of self and society in Fijian kindergarteners', *Ethos*, 37, 3, 314–33.

Bryant, C. (2010), 'Adolescence, pornography, and harm', *Youth Studies Australia*, 29, 1, 18–26.

Bryant, K. (2006), 'Making gender identity disorder of childhood: Historical lessons for contemporary debates', *Sexuality Research and Social Policy*, 3, 3, 23–39.

—, 'In defense of gay children? "progay" homophobia and the production of homonormativity', *Sexualities*, 11, 4, 455–75.

Buchmann, C., DiPrete, T. A. and McDaniel, A. (2008), 'Gender inequalities in education', *Annual Review of Sociology*, 34, 319–37.

Bühler-Niederberger, D. and Van Krieken, R. (2008), 'Persisting inequalities: Childhood between global influences and local traditions', *Childhood*, 15, 147–55.

Burns, K. (2008), '(re)Imagining the global, rethinking gender in education', *Discourse: Studies in the Cultural Politics of Education*, 29, 3, 343–57.

Carrington, V. and Hodgetts, K. (2010), 'Literacy-lite in BarbieGirls™', *British Journal of Sociology of Education*, 31, 6, 671–83.

Chan, P. (2006), '"No, it is not just a phase": An adolescent's right to sexual minority identity under the United Nations Convention on the Rights of the Child', *International Journal of Human Rights*, 10, 2, 161–76.

Chaudhuri, K. and Roy, S. (2009), 'Gender gap in educational attainment: Evidence from rural india', *Education Economics*, 17, 2, 215–38.

Chen, E. and Rao, N. (2011), 'Gender socialization in Chinese kindergartens: Teachers' contributions', *Sex Roles*, 64, 1/2, 103–16.

Cherney, I. and London, K. (2006), 'Gender-linked differences in the toys, television shows, computer games, and outdoor activities of 5 to 13-year-old children', *Sex Roles*, 54, 9/10, 717–26.

Choi, J. Y. and Lee, S. H. (2006), 'Does prenatal care increase access to child immunization?: Gender bias among children in India', *Social Science & Medicine*, 63, 1, 107–17.

Chu, C. Y. C, Tsay, R. S. and Yu, R. R. (2008), 'Intergenerational transmission of sex-specific differential treatments: The allocation of education resources among siblings', *Social Science Research*, 37, 2, 386–99.

Chung, S. K. (2007), 'Media/visual literacy art education: Sexism in hip-hop music videos', *Art Education*, 60, 3, 33–8.

Clarke, P. (2005), '"A nice little wife to make things pleasant": Portrayals of women in Canadian history textbooks approved in British Columbia', *McGill Journal of Education*, 40, 2, 241–65.

Clarke, V. and Kitzinger, C. (2005), '"We're not living on planet lesbian": Constructions of male role models in debates about lesbian families', *Sexualities*, 8, 2, 137–52.

Clearfield, M. W. and Nelson, N. M. (2006), 'Sex differences in mothers' speech and play behavior with 6-, 9-, and 14-month-old infants', *Sex Roles*, 54, 1/2, 127–37.

Connell, R. (1987), *Gender and power*. Stanford, CA: Stanford University Press.

— (1995), *Masculinities*. Berkeley, CA: University of California Press.

— (2010), 'Kartini's children: On the need for thinking gender and education together on a world scale', *Gender and Education*, 22, 6, 603–15.

Cook, D. T. and Kaiser, S. B. (2004), 'Betwixt and be tween: Age ambiguity and the sexualization of the female consuming subject', *Journal of Consumer Culture*, 4, 2, 203–27.

Corsaro, W. A. (2005), *The sociology of childhood*. Thousand Oaks, CA: Pine Forge Press.

Croll, E. J. (2006), 'From the girl child to girls' rights', *Third World Quarterly*, 27, 7, 1285–97.

Cunningham, M. (2001), 'Parental influences on the gendered division of housework', *American Sociological Review*, 66, 2, 184–203.

Currie, D. H., Kelly, D. M. and Pomerantz, S. (2007), '"The power to squash people": Understanding girls' relational aggression', *British Journal of Sociology of Education*, 28, 1, 23–37.

Dagkas, S. and Benn, T. (2006), 'Young Muslim women's experiences of Islam and physical education in Greece and Britain', *Sport, Education and Society*, 11, 1, 21–38.

D'Augelli, A. R., Grossman, A. H., Starks, M. T. and Sinclair, K. O. (2010), 'Factors associated with parents' knowledge of gay, lesbian, and bisexual youths' sexual orientation', *Journal of GLBT Family Studies*, 6, 2, 178–98.

Daley, A., Solomon, S., Newman, P. A. and Mishna, F. (2007), 'Traversing the margins: Intersectionalities in the bullying of lesbian, gay, bisexual and transgender youth', *Journal of Gay & Lesbian Social Services*, 19, 3/4, 9–29.

Davies, B. (1989), *Frogs and snails and feminist tales: Preschool children and gender*. Sydney, Australia: Allen & Unwin (2nd edn., 2003, Hampton Press).

— (2011), 'Open listening: Creative evolution in early childhood settings', *International Journal of Early Childhood*, 43, 2, 119–32.

Davies, B. and Kasama, H. (2004), *Gender in Japanese preschools*. Cresskill, NJ: Hampton Press.

Dennis, J. P. (2009), 'The boy who would be queen: Hints and closets on children's television', *Journal of Homosexuality*, 56, 6, 738–56.

— (2010), 'Drawing desire: Male youth and homoerotic fan art', *Journal of LGBT Youth*, 7, 1, 6–28.

DiIorio, C., Pluhar, E. and Belcher, L. (2003), 'Parent-child communication about sexuality: A review of the literature from 1980–2002', *Journal of HIV/AIDS Prevention & Education for Adolescents & Children*, 5, 3/4, 7–32.

Dubey, B. R. and Dubey, S. R. (1999), 'Child marriage in Rajasthan', *Development*, 42, 1, 75–7.

Dugmore, P. and Cocker, C. (2008), 'Legal, social and attitudinal changes: An exploration of lesbian and gay issues in a training programme for social workers in fostering and adoption', *Social Work Education*, 27, 159–68.

Dukmak, S. (2010), 'Classroom interaction in regular and special education middle primary classrooms in the United Arab Emirates', *British Journal of Special Education*, 37, 1, 39–48.

Dwairy, M., Achoui, M., Abouserie, R., Farah, A., Sakhleh, A., Fayad, M., and Khan, H. (2006), 'Parenting styles in Arab societies', *Journal of Cross-Cultural Psychology*, 37, 3, 230–47.

Edstrom, C. (2009), 'Preschool as an arena of gender policies: The examples of Sweden and Scotland', *European Educational Research Journal*, 8, 4, 534–49.

Egan, R. D. and Hawkes, G. L. (2008), 'Imperiled and perilous: Exploring the history of childhood sexuality', *Journal of Historical Sociology*, 21, 4, 355–67.

Elgar, A. G. (2004), 'Science textbooks for lower secondary schools in Brunei: Issues of gender equity', *International Journal of Science Education*, 26, 7, 875–94.

Elia, J. P. and Eliason, M. (2010), 'Discourses of exclusion: Sexuality education's silencing of sexual others', *Journal of LGBT Youth*, 7, 1, 29–48.

Esnaola, I., Rodriguez, A. and Goni, A. (2010), 'Body dissatisfaction and perceived sociocultural pressures', *Salud Mental*, 33, 1, 21–9.

Evaldsson, A. C. (2003), 'Throwing like a girl? Situating gender differences in physicality across game contexts', *Childhood*, 10, 4, 475–97.

Ewing Lee, E. and Troop-Gordon, W. (2011), 'Peer processes and gender role development', *Sex Roles*, 64, 1/2, 90–103.

Ezekiel, J. (2006), 'French dressing: Race, gender, and the hijab story', *Feminist Studies*, 32, 2, 256–78.

Ferfolja, T. (2007), 'Schooling cultures: Institutionalizing heteronormativity and heterosexism', *International Journal of Inclusive Education*, 11, 2, 147–62.

Fine, C. (2010), *Delusions of gender*, New York, NY: W.W. Norton.

Fingerson, L. (2006), 'Agency and the body in adolescent menstrual talk', *Childhood*, 12, 1, 91–110.

Fitzpatrick, M. and McPherson, B. (2010), 'Coloring within the lines: Gender stereotypes in contemporary coloring books', *Sex Roles*, 62, 1/2, 127–37.

Flicker, S., Travers, R., Flynn, S., Larkin, J., Guta, A., Salehi, R., Pole, J. D. and Layne, C. (2010), 'Sexual health research for and with urban youth', *Canadian Journal of Human Sexuality*, 19, 4, 133–44.

Furnham, A. and Saar, A. (2005), 'Gender-role stereotyping in adult and children's television advertisements: A two-study comparison between Great Britain and Poland', *Communications*, 30, 1, 73–91.

Galambos, N. L. and Martínez, M. L. (2007), 'Poised for emerging adulthood in Latin America', *Child Development Perspectives*, 1, 2, 109–14.

García, D. I., Gray-Stanley, J. and Ramirez-Valles, J. (2008), '"The priest obviously doesn't know that I'm gay": The religious and spiritual journeys of Latino gay men', *Journal of Homosexuality*, 55, 3, 411–36.

Gault-Sherman, M., Silver, E. and Sigfúsdóttir, I. D. (2009), 'Gender and the associated impairments of childhood sexual abuse', *Social Science & Medicine*, 69, 10, 1515–22.

Gerber, T. and Cheung, S. Y. (2008), 'Horizontal stratification in postsecondary education', *Annual Review of Sociology*, 34, 299–318.

Giordano, S. (2007), 'Gender atypical organisation in children and adolescents', *International Journal of Children's Rights*, 15, 365–90.

Global Partners in Action (2009), 'Youth: The call', Online: www.globalngoforum.de/youth

Gordon. M. K. (2008), 'Media contributions to African American girls' focus on beauty and appearance', *Psychology of Women Quarterly*, 32, 3, 245–56.

Gotz, M., Lemish, D., Aidman, A. and Moon, H. (2005), *Media and the make-believe worlds of children*. London, UK: Lawrence Erlbaum Associates.

Greany, K. (2008), 'Rhetoric versus reality: Exploring the rights-based approach to girls' education in Niger', *Compare: A Journal of Comparative Education*, 38, 5, 555–68.

Hall, C. (2005), 'Gender and boys' singing in early childhood', *British Journal of Music Education*, 22, 1, 5–20.

Hamilton, M. C., Anderson, D., Broaddus, M. and Young, K. (2006), 'Gender stereotyping and under-representation of female characters in 200 popular children's picture books: A twenty-first century update', *Sex Roles*, 55, 11/12, 757–65.

Hartley, B. and Sutton, R. (2010), 'Children's development of stereotypical gender-related expectations about academic engagement and consequences for performance', Paper presented at the British Educational Research Association annual conference, University of Warwick, Coventry, UK.

Hicks, S. (2008), 'Gender role models . . . who needs 'em?', *Qualitative Social Work*, 7, 1, 43–59.

Honkatukia, P., Nyqvist, L. and Pösö, T. (2007), 'Violence talk and gender in youth residential care', *Journal of Scandinavian Studies in Criminology & Crime Prevention*, 8, 1, 56–76.

Horn, S. S., Kosciw, J. G. and Russell, S. T. (2009), 'New research on lesbian, gay, bisexual, and transgender youth', *Journal of Youth and Adolescence*, 38, 863–6.

Hosein, G. J. (2007), 'Survival stories: Challenges facing youth in Trinidad and Tobago', *Race & Class*, 49, 2, 125–30.

Hunt, K. (2009), 'Saving the children: (Queer) youth sexuality and the age of consent in Canada', *Sexuality Research & Social Policy*, 6, 3, 15–33.

Hurley, D. (2005), 'Seeing white: Children of color and the Disney fairy tale princess', *Journal of Negro Education*, 74, 3, 221–32.

Hust, S. J., Brown, J. and L'Engle, K. L. (2008), 'Boys will be boys and girls better be prepared: An analysis of rare sexual health messages in young adolescents' media', *Mass Communication & Society*, 11, 1, 3–23.

Hyde, A., Carney, M., Drennan, J., Butler, M., Lohan, M. and Howlett, E. (2010), 'The silent treatment: Parents' narratives of sexuality education with young people', *Culture, Health & Sexuality*, 12, 4, 359–71.

Izugbara, C. O. (2005), 'Local erotic songs and chants among rural Nigerian adolescent males', *Sexuality & Culture*, 9, 3, 53–76.

Jackson, C. and Dempster, S. (2009), '"I sat back on my computer . . . with a bottle of whisky next to me": constructing "cool" masculinity through "effortless" achievement in secondary and higher education', *Journal of Gender Studies*, 18, 4, 341–56.

Jacquemin, M. (2006), 'Can the language of rights get hold of the complex realities of child domestic work?' *Childhood*, 13, 3, 389–406.

James, A. and James, A. (2008), *Key concepts in childhood studies*. London: Sage.

Johnson, D. (2007), '"This is political!": Negotiating the legacies of the first school-based gay youth group', *Children, Youth and Environments*, 17, 2, 380–7.

Jones, D. C., and Crawford, J. K. (2006), 'The peer appearance culture during adolescence', *Journal of Youth & Adolescence*, 35, 2, 243–55.

Jones, P. and Welch, S. (2010), *Rethinking children's rights: Attitudes in contemporary society*. London: Continuum International.

Jordan, E. and Cowan, A. (1995), 'Warrior narratives in the kindergarten classroom', *Gender & Society*, 9, 6, 727–43.

Joshi, S., Peter, J. and Valkenburg, P. (2011), 'Scripts of sexual desire and danger in US and Dutch teen girl magazines', *Sex Roles*, 64, 7/8, 463–74.

Kaestle, C. E., Halpern, C. T. and Brown, J. D. (2007), 'Music videos, pro wrestling, and acceptance of date rape among middle school males and females', *Journal of Adolescent Health*, 40, 185–7.

Kane, E. W. (2006), '"No way my boys are going to be like that!": Parents' responses to children's gender nonconformity', *Gender & Society*, 20, 2, 149–76.

— (2009), '"I wanted a soul mate": Gendered anticipation and frameworks of accountability in parents' preferences for sons and daughters', *Symbolic Interaction,* 32, 4, 372–89.

Karniol, R. (2009), 'Israeli kindergarten children's gender constancy for others' counter-stereotypic toy play and appearance', *Infant and Child Development*, 18, 1, 73–94.

Karsten, L. (2003), 'Children's use of public space: The gendered world of the playground', *Childhood*, 10, 4, 457–73.

Keddie, A. (2003), 'Little boys: Tomorrow's macho lads', *Discourse: Studies in the Cultural Politics of Education*, 24, 3, 289–306.

— (2009), 'National gender equity and schooling policy in Australia', *Australian Educational Researcher*, 36, 2, 21–37.

Kelly, D., Pomeranz, S. and Currie, D. (2005), 'Skater girlhood and emphasized femininity: "You can't land an ollie properly in heels"', *Gender & Education*, 17, 3, 229–48.

Kosmisnsky, E. and Daniel, L. (2005), 'Toys and games: Childhood in the Parque das NaÇões Favela in Brazil', *Sociological Studies of Children and Youth*, 10, 23–41.

Krafchick, J. L., Zimmerman, T. S., Haddock, S. A. and Banning, J. H. (2005), 'Best-selling books advising parents about gender', *Family Relations*, 54, 1, 84–100.

Kumashiro, K., Baber, S. A., Richardson, E., Ricker-Wilson, C. and Wong, P. L. (2004), 'Preparing teachers for anti-oppressive education', *Teaching Education*, 15, 3, 257–75.

Kyratzis, A. and Guo, J. (2001), 'Preschool girls' and boys' verbal conflict strategies in the United States and China', *Research on Language & Social Interaction*, 34, 1, 45–74.

Kyratzis, A. And Tarim, S. D. (2010), 'Using directives to construct egalitarian or hierarchical social organization', *First Language*, 30, 3–4, 473–92.

Laborde, C. (2006), 'Female autonomy, education, and the hijab', *Critical Review of International Social and Political Philosophy*, 9, 3, 351–77.

Lacroix, C. (2004), 'Images of animated others: The orientalization of Disney's cartoon heroines', *Popular Communication*, 2, 4, 213–29.

Lamb, L. M., Bigler, R. S., Liben, L. S. and Green, V. A. (2009), 'Teaching children to confront peers' sexist remarks', *Sex Roles*, 61, 5/6, 361–82.

Langer. S. and Martin, J. (2004), 'How dresses can make you mentally ill: Examining gender identity disorder in children', *Child and Adolescent Social Work Journal*, 21, 1, 5–23.

Leach, F. (2003), 'Learning to be violent: The role of the school in developing adolescent gendered behaviour', *Compare*, 33, 3, 385–400.

Lee, L. (2008), 'Understanding gender through Disney's marriages: A study of young Korean immigrant girls', *Early Childhood Education Journal*, 36, 1, 11–18.

Levison, D. and Moe, K. (1998), 'Household work as a deterrent to schooling: An analysis of adolescent girls in Peru', *Journal of Developing Areas*, 32, 3, 339–56.

Lewin-Jones, J. and Mitra, B. (2009), 'Gender roles in television commercials and primary school children in the UK', *Journal of Children & Media*, 3, 1, 35–51.

Lubbe, C. (2008), 'The experiences of children growing up in lesbian-headed families in South Africa', *Journal of GLBT Family Studies*, 4, 3, 325–59.

Luria, Z., Provenzano, F. J, and Rubin, J. Z. (1974). 'The Eye of the beholder: Parents' views on sex of newborns', *American Journal of Orthopsychiatry*, 44, 512–19.

MacIntosh, L. (2007), 'Gay-straight alliances: From frontline to bottom line', *Journal of Curriculum & Pedagogy*, 4, 2, 130–5.

Maglajliá, R. A. and Tiffany, J. (2006), 'Participatory action research with youth in Bosnia and Herzegovina', *Journal of Community Practice*, 14, 1/2, 163–81.

Martin, K. A. (1998), 'Becoming a gendered body: Practices of preschools', *American Sociological Review*, 63, 4, 494–511.

Martin, K. A. and Kazyak, E. (2009), 'Hetero-romantic love and heterosexiness in children's G-rated films', *Gender & Society*, 23, 3, 315–36.

Martin, K. A. and Luke, K. (2010), 'Gender differences in the ABC's of the birds and the bees: What mothers teach young children about sexuality and reproduction', *Sex Roles*, 62, 3/4, 278–91.

Martin, K. A., Luke, K. P. and Verduzco-Baker, L. (2007), 'The sexual socialization of young children', *Advances in Group Processes*, 24, 231–59.

Martin, K. A., Hutson, D. J., Kazyak, E. and Scherrer, K. S. (2010), 'Advice when children come out: The cultural "tool kits" of parents', *Journal of Family Issues*, 31, 7, 960–91.

Massengale, D. and Lough, N. (2010), 'Women leaders in sport: Where's the gender equity?' *The Journal of Physical Education, Recreation & Dance*, 81, 4, 6–8.

Mbilizi, M. A. (2008), 'In two different worlds: How Malawian girls experience schooling', *Journal of International Women's Studies*, 9, 3, 223–40.

McGuffey, C. S. (2008), '"Saving masculinity": Gender reaffirmation, sexuality, race, and parental responses to male child sexual abuse', *Social Problems*, 55, 2, 216–37.

McGuffey, C. S. and Rich, B. L. (1999), 'Playing in the gender transgression zone', *Gender & Society*, 13, 5, 608–27.

McHale, S. M., Crouter, A. C. and Whiteman, S. W. (2003), 'The family context of gender development in childhood and adolescence', *Social Development*, 12, 1, 125–48.

Meadow, T. (2011), '"Deep down where the music plays": How parents account for childhood gender variance', *Sexualities*, 14, 6, 725–47.

Meyer, E. (2008), 'Gendered harassment in secondary schools: Understanding teachers' (non) interventions', *Gender & Education*, 20, 6, 555–70.

Meyouhas, T. (2010), 'Sexual harassment in education', *Georgetown Journal of Gender & the Law*, 11, 1, 297–313.

Minks, A. (2008), 'Performing gender in song games among Nicaraguan Miskitu children', *Language & Communication*, 28, 1, 36–56.

Montgomery, H. (2005), 'Gendered childhoods: A cross disciplinary overview', *Gender and Education*, 17, 471–82.

— (2010), 'Focusing on the child, not the prostitute', *Wagadu: Journal of Transnational Women's & Gender Studies*, 8, 166–88.

Morrow, V. (2006), 'Understanding gender differences in context', *Children & Society*, 20, 2, 92–104.

Myers, K. and Raymond, L. (2010), 'Elementary school girls and heteronormativity', *Gender & Society*, 24, 2, 167–88.

Nam, K., Lee, G. and Hwang, J. (2011), 'Gender stereotypes depicted by western and Korean advertising models in Korean adolescent girls magazines', *Sex Roles*, 64, 3/4, 223–37.

Neto, F. and Furnham, A. (2005), 'Gender-role portrayals in children's television advertisements', *International Journal of Adolescence and Youth*, 12, 1–2, 69–90.

Nielsen, H. B. (2004), 'European gender lessons: Girls and boys at scout camps in Denmark, Portugal, Russia and Slovakia', *Childhood*, 11, 2, 207–26.

Okkolin, M. A., Lehtomäki, E. and Bhalalusesa, E. (2010), 'The successful education sector development in Tanzania-comment on gender balance and inclusive education', *Gender & Education*, 22, 1, 63–71.

Pande, R. (2003), 'Selective gender differences in childhood nutrition and immunization in rural India', *Demography*, 40, 3, 395–418.

Parker, L. H. and Rennie, L. J. (2002), 'Teachers' implementation of gender-inclusive instructional strategies in single-sex and mixed-sex science classrooms', *International Journal of Science Education*, 24, 9, 881–97.

Pascoe, C. J. (2007), *Dude, you're a fag: Masculinity and sexuality in high school*. Berkeley, CA: University of California Press.

Peters, B. M. (2010), 'Emo gay boys and subculture: Postpunk queer youth and (re)thinking images of masculinity', *Journal of LGBT Youth*, 7, 2, 129–46.

Pfaff, N. (2010), 'Gender segregation in pre-adolescent peer groups as a matter of class', *Childhood*, 17, 1, 43–60.

Phillips, B. and Phillips, D. A. (2010), 'Learning from youth exposed to domestic violence: Decentering DV and the primacy of gender stereotypes', *Violence Against Women*, 16, 3, 291–312.

Portelli, J. (2006), 'Language: An important signifier of masculinity in a bilingual context', *Gender & Education*, 18, 4, 413–30.

Raley, S. and Bianchi, S. (2006), 'Sons, daughters, and family processes: Does gender of children matter?' *Annual Review of Sociology*, 32, 401–21.

Reay, D. (2001), '"Spice girls", "nice girls", "girlies", and "tomboys": Gender discourses, girls' cultures and femininities in the primary classroom', *Gender & Education*, 13, 2, 153–66.

Reed, B. W., Cohen-Kettenis, P. T., Reed, T. and Spack, N. (2008), 'Medical care for gender variant young people', *Sexologies*, 17, 4, 258–65.

Renold, E. (2007), 'Primary schools "studs"', *Men and Masculinities*, 9, 3, 275–97.

Rice, E. H., Merves, E. and Srsic, A. (2008), 'Perceptions of gender differences in the expression of emotional and behavioral disabilities', *Education and Treatment of Children*, 31, 4, 549–65.

Riggs, D. W. (2008), 'All the boys are straight: Heteronormativity in contemporary books on fathering and raising sons', *Thymos: Journal of Boyhood Studies*, 2, 186–202.

Risman, B. (1998), *Gender vertigo*. New Haven: Yale University Press.

Robinson, K. H. (2005), 'Reinforcing hegemonic masculinities through sexual harassment', *Gender and Education*, 17, 1, 19–37.

Robinson, K. H. and Davies, C. (2008), 'She's kickin' ass, that's what she's doing!' *Australian Feminist Studies*, 23, 57, 343–58.

Robson, E. (2004), 'Children at work in rural Northern Nigeria', *Journal of Rural Studies*, 20, 2, 193–210.

Rogers, C. (2009), '(S)excerpts from a life told: Sex, gender, and learning disability', *Sexualities*, 12, 3, 270–88.

Rosario, M., Schrimshaw, E. and Hunter, J. (2004), 'Ethnic/racial differences in the coming-out processes of lesbian, gay, and bisexual youths', *Cultural Diversity and Ethnic Minority Psychology*, 10, 3, 215–28.

Røthing, Å. (2008), 'Homotolerance and heteronormativity in Norwegian classrooms', *Gender and Education*, 20, 3, 253–66.

Russell, R. and Tyler, M. (2005), 'Branding and bricolage: Gender, consumption and transition', *Childhood*, 12, 2, 221–37.

Rydstrøm, H. (2006), 'Masculinity and punishment: Men's upbringing of boys in rural Vietnam', *Childhood*, 13, 3, 329–48.

Rysst, M. (2010), '"I am only 10 years old": Femininities, clothing-fashion codes and the intergenerational gap of interpretation of young girls' clothes', *Childhood*, 17, 1, 76–93.

Seaman, A. and DeJean, W. (2010), 'Editorial', *Australasian Journal of Early Childhood*, 35, 1, i–iii.

Selfhout, M. H., Delsing, M. J. M. H., ter Bogt, T. F. M. and Meeus, W. H. J. (2008), 'Heavy metal and hip-hop style preferences and externalizing problem behavior', *Youth & Society*, 39, 4, 435–52.

Sengupta, R. (2006), 'Reading representations of black, east Asian, and white women in magazines for adolescent girls', *Sex Roles*, 54, 11/12, 799–808.

Shanahan, S. (2007), 'Lost and found: The sociological ambivalence toward childhood', *Annual Review of Sociology*, 33, 407–28.

Stacey, J. and Biblarz, T. J. (2001), '(How) does the sexual orientation of parents matter?' *American Sociological Review*, 66, 2, 159–83.

Stevens, M., Golombok, S. and Beveridge, M. (2002), 'Does father absence influence children's gender development?' *Parenting: Science and Practice*, 2, 1, 47–60.

Sullivan, A. (2009), 'Academic self-concept, gender and single-sex schooling', *British Educational Research Journal*, 35, 2, 259–88.

Sultana, R. G. (2008), 'Implementing the gender equity initiative in the MENA region', *Mediterranean Journal of Educational Studies*, 13, 1, 125–36.

Švab, A. (2007), 'New ways of parenting: Fatherhood and parenthood in lesbian families', *Revija za Sociologiju*, 38, 1/2, 43–55.

Taft, J. (2010), *Rebel girls*. New York, NY: New York University Press.

Teixeira, A. B. M., Villani, C. and do Nascimento, S. (2008), 'Exploring modes of communication among pupils in Brazil: Gender issues in academic performance', *Gender & Education*, 20, 4, 387–98.

Tenenbaum, H. R., Hill, D. B., Joseph, N. and Roche, E. (2010), '"It's a boy because he's painting a picture": Age differences in children's conventional and unconventional gender schemas', *British Journal of Psychology*, 101, 1, 137–54.

Thorne, B. (1993), *Gender play*. New Brunswick, NJ: Rutgers University Press.

Turner, S. (1999), 'Intersex identities: Locating new intersections of sex and gender', *Gender & Society*, 13, 4, 457–79.

UNICEF (2010a), 'Fact Sheet: A Summary of the Rights Under the Convention on the Rights of the Child', Online: www.unicef.org/crc/files/Rights_overview.pdf.

— (2010b), 'Fact Sheet: The Rights of Girls', Online: www.unicef.org/crc/files/Rights_of_girls.pdf.

van Putten, A. E., Dykstra, P. A. and Schippers, J. J. (2008), 'Just like mom?: The intergenerational reproduction of women's paid work', *European Sociological Review*, 24, 4, 435–49.

Vekiri, I. and Chronaki, A. (2008), 'Gender issues in technology use: Perceived social support, computer self-efficacy and value beliefs, and computer use beyond school', *Computers & Education*, 51, 3, 1392–404.

Wallien, M., Veenstra, R., Kreukels, B. and Cohen-Kettenis, P. (2010), 'Peer group status of gender dysphoric children', *Archives of Sexual Behavior*, 39, 2, 553–60.

Walters, J. and McNeely, C. (2010), 'Recasting Title IX: Addressing gender equity in the science, technology, engineering, and mathematics professoriate', *Review of Policy Research*, 27, 3, 317–32.

West, C. and Zimmerman, D. (1987), 'Doing gender', *Gender & Society*, 1, 124–51.

Williams, D., Martins, N., Consalvo, M. and Ivory, J. D. (2009), 'The virtual census: Representations of gender, race and age in video games', *New Media & Society*, 11, 5, 815–34.

Wood, E., Desmarais, S. and Gugula, S. (2002), 'The impact of parenting experience on gender stereotyped toy play of children', *Sex Roles*, 47, 1/2, 39–49.

Yu, L. and Xie, D. (2010), 'Multidimensional gender identity and psychological adjustment in middle childhood', *Sex Roles*, 62, 1/2, 100–13.

Index